Snapshots of History. Through the Lavender Keyhole

ISBN: 1-4791-7590-0
ISBN-13: 9781479175901

Snapshots of History. Through the Lavender Keyhole

Older Lesbians Share Their Stories

Darlene K. Bogle

Dedication

This Book is dedicated to my Partner for Life,
Becky Lake.
Thank you honey for your support, love and kindness as I
strive to create a book that honors the journey of
our lesbian sisterhood.

Acknowledgments

Although writing is a solitary act, no book is written by one individual. Thank you my sisters for trusting me with your stories, for listening to my process as I struggled to be true to your journey. Thank you for the suggestions for a book title, (Karen Mackey) and for encouraging me in the process. My heart is full as I have lived with your experiences, and felt your pain.

Thank you Kat Silver for the photo that graces the front of my book! Your creativity is awesome. To see more, or to contact Kat:
CREATIONS BY KAT
Art & Travel Photography
Website: www.kat-silver.com
Email: kat-silver@hotmail.com

Thank you, Marlie Heberling. You did an amazing job of producing the graphics for the book cover.

We are all part of history...Kate Clinton

Forward

The stories that follow in this book, accomplish two things. They tell about our history as we look back on events. They also tell about our future, as they leave a memory for younger generations. These stories should inspire every reader with the realization that LGBT folks have been, and continue to be a part of history.

Darlene is a listener. She walked in my shoes for over a year, writing the story of my life: <u>A Miracle Woman, The Naomi Harvey Story</u>. She is like a sister to me. She is interested in the stories that each woman has to share. Many of these women would never tell their stories and share the bits of their lives had Darlene not taken an interest.

She has a heart to lift and encourage others. Her caring and compassion come through in these stories that span over sixty years. Some of these women have great faith and are strong women. However, all of them share the experience of being who they are as lesbians in a world where it was not always safe to be "out."

A few of these women still find it difficult to speak openly about who they are, while others are outspoken activists. Darlene shares how each of us is woven into the fabric of society and each one is needed to stand and declare the sisterhood bond we all share.

We are many voices, yet one message:
We were there.
We are here.
We will stand with you in the future.

Naomi Harvey

Introduction

Now that we have reached the age where we are considered seniors, we have been assigned a new responsibility that is to share our lives with others and make our presence known within a largely heterosexual society. Ours is not solely the right to obtain senior discounts, but includes that of keeping a flame of our lesbian history alive for new generations to read.

I realize this responsibility has also now fallen to me. Recording my family history, as well as others in the history of the Lesbian and Gay community has become a passion. I realize that so many events that were part of my life experience are now talked about on the history channel. I grew up in the sixties in the San Francisco Bay area. I walked along the streets of Haight/Ashbury and hung out in People's Park in Berkeley. If I had known I was part of historic events, I would have taken better notes.

Thankfully, I have been blessed with a broad spectrum of friendships with women who have trusted me enough to share their history. I am forever changed.

On New Year's Eve in 2009, a small group of professional women gathered for a meal at the home of one couple. Most of us knew each other, having shared many meals, basketball games, holiday celebrations and other social events over the years.

Our assignment that evening was to bring some small items that represented "time" to us and to share that history with the group. I listened quietly as pictures were revealed with stories of childhood, or a journal from a favorite relative was passed around the group. No matter that it was in a foreign language that none of us could read. It was part of her family history.

The stories brought some laughter, some tears, and a huge question for me (posed by my friend, Jeanne De Joseph). "Who will know these parts of us when we have no children or heirs to remember? We may be the last generation of our family, and the richness of our past will fall silent with our passing."

My life has brought me into contact with some amazing women. I am honored to call them friends, and to listen to their stories. This compilation of events is not meant to be a historical telling of the influence of lesbians throughout the twentieth century, but snapshots of lives that have been lived mostly in obscurity. Most of these women are not famous, and have no desire to be on the six o'clock news. The flame of passion is burning strong and bright in their lives. We will not submit to being women who are devalued by a patriarchal society or forced to fade away as if we never lived.

I have observed the lives of lesbians in the twenty first century through the lens of my own coming out and being public. I was surprised to discover that my experiences are not the case for every lesbian. (Imagine! The world doesn't revolve around my concepts and understanding of how "Lesbiana" should be portrayed.)

A huge segment of our society is still private, reserved and hesitant to stand on a street corner in their home towns with signs promoting gay rights. It's not that they do not support equality, but the reality is that for our community as well as other minorities, Equality is not a reality. The opposition to who we are is quite evident in politics and religion. Each year brings an increasing number of hate crimes. Many churches and families still reject the lesbian aunt or sister. Gay jokes are still viewed as an acceptable form of humor on late night television or the men's locker room.

I have become more of an outspoken activist as I have entered into my senior years. I enjoy the interaction, and sometimes conflict with those who want to debate whether God's loving acceptance is extended to all His children, including his Gay and Lesbian children.

I have found that friendships with heterosexual women are often not as comfortable as those with lesbians. It's not that I don't like heterosexuals; however there is bond that is shared in "sisterhood". Equality, although desired, cannot be achieved by popular vote. The women whose stories I share are either retired, or almost ready to retire. Their support base has been formed through years of cautious revelation of their private lives. They no longer fear termination of their jobs at this stage of their lives; however, rejection is a silent fear.

I have been amazed to discover that in the entire history making events in our world, many of my lesbian sisters were making their own history, which was then, weaved into the fabric of history of the world.

I think it's important to show that most of the time, they were unaware of the historic value of their presence in that "event". Whether serving together in battles, marching for civil rights, or just taking a stand for equality and calling for an end to oppression. Lesbians have always been there.

The other discovery is that so many of the women are still held in bondage of fear that who they are today can still be impacted by the revelation of their sexual identity. Many of the women I spoke with were hesitant to have their name in print. While I understand that fear, it is sad to me that women must still deal with that fear of exposure.

The women you meet on these pages come from all walks of life and levels of education. Their journeys' of self discovery are shared in the hope that the mere fact that they lived, is reason enough to celebrate.

I believe that we are all changed in the depth of our soul when we listen to the stories of these women who have been part of history, or who are making history. We might not think that we are changed, however each story is part of our own. We cannot journey through life untouched by those who have traveled before us, or those who walk with us. There is also a generation what will come after us, and are looking for role models.

I didn't always understand this concept and mostly surrounded myself with women who shared similar beliefs of faith and economic values. I often intellectually dismissed those who were different, especially in the area of faith.

I realize now that my flame was diminished and my knowing was limited. It still is, in many ways because change does not come easy to my heart, and there are so many aspects of my evangelical Christian teachings that are deeply imbedded in my thinking. I have been robbed of the richness of "other" by thinking they were somehow not acceptable to my God. I have come to understand that we are all God's children, and wherever we are on life's journey, even if we follow no particular faith practice, God is greater than my ability to understand or define Him. This awareness has transformed my own journey.

Each of these women has caused me to examine my part in the stewardship of recording and sharing stories. The fragile emotions; the strength of resolve to not be forgotten by a world where sometimes fifteen minutes of fame goes only to the bizarre actions of an outrageous individual. My world is filled with women who might never be noticed or make the nightly news. The majority of them are not social justice activists and although they have strong beliefs, they live their lives in the ordinary.

I have found another group of women who stand with their lesbian sisters hand in hand, and speak out for equality. These are heterosexual allies who lead the way in speaking out for equality. They have a deep commitment to promoting equality for everyone, and speak out on a national level calling for the right of LGBT folks to be included as equals. They are given a voice through such groups at PFLAG. My life is enriched and challenged as I stand with them upon a world stage, unashamed of the woman God created me to be. I am accepted as an equal and strong voice for equality.

I remember one advocate telling me that heterosexuals who stand for gay rights also have a coming out process. They experience similar rejection from family and church, and many times, loss of jobs and income. Is it any wonder that so many within the gay community are hesitant to speak out their truth?

I attend a church that is open and affirming, and supporting of equality for the gay community. My spouse and I are accepted, welcomed and involved in all aspects our church family. I am humbled that people, who have no personal obligation to speak out, are doing so, just because it is the right thing. I no longer feel isolated in my journey to bring awareness and acceptance of lesbian and gay persons in our world. Sharing these snapshots of history is just one way of proclaiming:
we were there-
-and we will always be there-
when history is recorded.

Some of the women I have met and listened to over the past couple of years have their stories recorded in these pages. There are many who have decided not to share their lives in print.

The women who have made a difference in our community are not always the ones who have their name on the front pages or find themselves featured on the local news casts.

There are women who work behind the scenes of political groups, or community resource centers for the LGBT communities. Many of these women work in regular jobs, living in committed relationships and yet they make a difference in our society just because they reflect the common influence of being a lesbian in a heterosexual world.

If you were to meet many of these women at a social gathering, the reaction is not, "Oh, I met a lesbian today," but I met a teacher, or a nurse, or an attorney today, and had a wonderful conversation. There is nothing to indicate that we are unique in society. We are however, part of the tapestry of every community, and have made contributions to every generation. May it continue to be so.

Darlene Bogle-Author/Activist
A Christian Lesbian Journey
A Miracle Woman, the Naomi Harvey Story.

Table of Contents

Chapter 1
Lesbian pioneers

Phyllis Lyon
70 plus

Any account of 20th century Lesbian history would of necessity include the names of Phyllis Lyon and Del Martin. Since the early 1950's they took a courageous stand as a lesbian couple who made no apologies for their love.

Although Del Martin passed away in August 2008, the legacy they forged together was not only written in the headlines, but upon the hearts of the gay community. They were together over 50 years, married in 2004 in San Francisco when Mayor Gavin Newsom allowed same sex couples to marry, and again on June 16th 2008 when the state declared same sex marriage legal. They were the first lesbian couple to marry on the steps of city hall.

On May 23, 2009, Phyllis was celebrated by the Women's International League for Peace and Freedom as one of the courageous women of the gay rights movement. She was interviewed by Rev. Deborah Johnson of Inner Light Ministries of Santa Cruz, California. Rev. Johnson is another courageous activist and spokesperson for gay rights. The interview included the following account:

The list of credits for Phyllis and Del read like a who's who for Lesbian awareness. They met in Seattle while on assignment with the Pacific Builders and Engineers. Phyllis was the associate editor to their publication. She had been working in Chico and accepted the Seattle job to expand her world.

She remembers the day the new editor was named. A good looking woman arrived carrying a briefcase and Phyllis was immediately intrigued. She had never seen a woman in a suit with a brief case. Over drinks with several co workers, the conversation turned to homosexuality, a topic which no one seemed to have much information. That is, besides Del Martin. Phyllis asked how it was that she knew so much on this topic, and Del responded, "Because I am one!"

They began to spend time together at the Journalist Press Club, as it was the only late night option for drinks due to Washington States' Blue laws. Initially, they were just friends; however Phyllis was comfortable with Del and enjoyed her company. After several months, Phyllis decided to move back to the San Francisco Bay area. She wanted to take a cross country trip with her sister, before she secured another job.

This was before the days of telephone calling cards and cell phones, but each day Phyllis would call "collect" to check in with Del. She found comfort in their conversations and Del encouraged her to "come home". Del had also returned to San Francisco and wanted Phyllis to move in with her and live as a couple.

The decision was made for her, when her sister became quite ill and was hospitalized. After many tests, they determined that she had polio. The trip was cut short, and Phyllis returned after a month. She wrote Del a letter and said, "Let's give this a try." She had been involved with men and said she didn't realize until Del, that women were an option. They moved in together to a small apartment on Castro Street in 1953

Rev. Deborah Johnson asked how they found other lesbians in those days. Phyllis recalled that they frequented a lot of lesbian bars in San Francisco, looking for friends. It was difficult, as most of the women were in clicks and not very friendly. They met a couple of gay men who were more open to social occasions, than the women at the bars.

After being together for three years, they got together with three other couples and founded the "secret club", the Daughters of Bilitis (DOB) in 1955. They wanted to have a social and political network organization for lesbians across the United States. Together, they were joint president and editors of the newsletter, "The Ladder". It was distributed locally at first, and later became the first lesbian publication as a resource for women looking for friendships with other lesbians. There was a small fee to join the organization and receive the newsletter.

Phyllis and Del were the first lesbian couple to join the National Organization for Women in the early 1960's. They insisted on the couple's rate.

Rev. Johnson asked Phyllis if she had any secrets for longevity in relationships, as they had such a long history.

Phyllis smiled and chuckled. "Just stay there, even if you have disagreements." She went on to share that a friend had given them a little kitten when they first got together, and kitten kept them together, because neither was willing to part with it! "We had arguments, and sometimes walked out the door and around the block, but we were committed, and you have to work things out."

She continued to share that when they purchased their first home in San Francisco for $11,000 in 1955, everyone knew they were a couple. The realtor was accepting of them and encouraged them to refer other "people like them" for home purchase. The home was larger than the apartment where they had started life together, and they soon added a new kitty to the family. That was almost a guarantee that they couldn't break up!

Rev. Johnson smiled and leaned forward. "Years ago, this platform was used as a church that supported Exodus International and tried to tell gays and lesbians that they had to change their lives to be acceptable. We've come a long way since then, and today we can declare that all God's people are loved and accepted. Did you ever experience religious persecution for being a lesbian couple?"

Her response was immediate. "I was never religious, so I didn't have all that baggage."

Rev. Johnson responded with emotional intensity. "I came from a deeply religious, Pentecostal background and was told almost daily that something was wrong with me and that I was a sinner and psychologically flawed." She paused, picking up a book from the table. "I was 16 years old when I found this book, _Lesbian Woman._ You literally saved my life. It was the first time ever that I had read that two women could love one another, and that it was OK. Thank you for writing this book all those years ago. I'm sure I'm not the only one who has been touched by reading it."

Amid the applause of the audience Rev. Deborah leaned toward Phyllis once again. "Since the 70's, you and Del were involved with many social Justice Groups and issues that pertained to lesbians. How did you get so involved in those areas?"

Phyllis thought for a moment, and then responded. "It was by accident mostly! I always thought it was because we were Democrats. We met so many women politicians who became our friends."

She continued, "The DOB was both a social and political voice for lesbians. We worked to form the Council of Religion and Homosexuality in northern California and sought to decriminalize homosexuality in the 1960's and early 70's. We were part of San Francisco's first gay political organization, the Alice B. Toklas Democratic Club, which influenced Dianne Feinstein to sponsor a citywide bill to outlaw employment discrimination for gays and lesbians. In 1995 we both served on the White House Conference on aging." She paused. "One of the most interesting women we met was Dr. Evelyn Hooker, from Southern California. She's passed on now, but she was the primary researcher responsible for having homosexuality removed from the Diagnostic and Statistical Manual of Mental Disorders (DSM) as a psychological disorder. We were in the right place and time to support those changes. Dr. Hooker was a straight woman who took up for the gay community."

Rev. Johnson asked another question. "What about your family? Did they support you as a lesbian couple? How did you tell them?"

Phyllis chuckled. "We never had that conversation. It was too much trouble to try and explain who we were. We were always together and figured it wasn't an issue."

Rev. Deborah smiled. "Well, one last question. Looking back what would you do over, if you had the chance?"

Phyllis smiled. "I think I could have gotten along without drinking so much! Other than that, I'm happy with my life."

"Thank you so much for being here today and being part of our conversation. You are a most courageous woman and thank you for all you have done in support of Lesbians around the country!" Rev. Deborah embraced Phyllis. "I've waited a long time for this. Would you do me the honor of autographing my book?"

The following half hour was filled with questions from the audience, and affirmations of the influence of Phyllis Lyon and Del Martin upon the community.

I left the auditorium feeling a deep appreciation for this pioneer of l lesbian rights, and a new determination to keep on my own journey of who I am, and let history determine if I made a difference.

Chapter 2
Butch or Femme

Shirley Sarten
Age 70 +

An outgoing woman in her early seventies, she bubbles with enthusiasm. She lives alone, with her two dogs. She is filled with the memories of former lovers, some deceased, some who moved on to other relationships. She values the friendships that helped form her life and told me that nothing is more important than long term relationships.

At first encounter, this strongly opinionated and outspoken woman might appear a bit tough and rough around the edges. She talks longingly of her appreciation of the "lipstick lesbian" woman. Shirley grew up in an era where roles were cherished and butch and femme were clearly defined. Shirley preferred women who were pleasing to the eye and more refined in their manners. Her early years had their share of bar room romance, but that now is a fading memory.

Two long term relationships are the significant influences in her life.

In her early 20's, she married a man, because it was the thing to do. She had two daughters and discovered she was not cut out to be a wife. She got a divorce, and her daughters were raised by her mother. They were not told about Shirley's lesbian lovers.

One lover spilled the beans during a visit with one of her daughters. Shirley's fear of rejection was then a moot point, as the daughter accepted her mother for who she was. "Everything makes sense now," was the immediate response.

Shirley worked over 30 years for the same factory in the city of Oakland. She was a hard worker and her small frame is still quite muscular because of all the years of "man's work". She embraces a strong work ethic, and those qualities carry over to her relationships.

She values friendships, and has had many that have spanned her lifetime. Many were with women preachers. She considers herself a religious person with a strong faith in God. She doesn't attend church every week, but prays and supports many who are in evangelism. One of those preachers is Naomi Harvey. Her story is told in (A Miracle Woman-the Naomi Harvey Story.)

Shirley has a twinkle in her eyes as she insists that she is not a "churchy" person, but that no way impacts her belief in God. Recently she underwent surgery for a knee replacement, and she was quick to call for this preacher to come be with her and pray for the surgery to be a success. I was happy to share that part of her journey, and thought to myself how much better the world would be if more people were less "churchy" and more open to a God experience in every aspect of life

Shirley is like so many of the older women I've spoken with over the past couple of years. She is not ashamed of being a Lesbian, but is not "out". She is a strong supporter of those who are out doing the work for Justice, but still carries the fear that for her to be vocal would mean rejection from those around her. That experience is not new with a current generation that is subjected to not only rejection, but acts of bullying. The desire to be loved and valued for who we are has been part of our core makeup for as long as people have recognized diversity. There are loud voices in society, both religious and political, that continue to diminish our value and personhood. There are also voices within the Gay and Lesbian community that are speaking out, proclaiming acceptance. Our message continues to be that we have contributions to make, and significance in this world just because of the fact that we exist.

Chapter 3
West Coast Stonewall

Mary Williamson-68
Retired-Southern California

Mary has been in an interracial relationship for twenty three years. She feels that she has been isolated from friendships because her lover is African-American. She was excluded from conversations and events because she didn't "fit in".

Mary feels that she knew from the age of ten or eleven that she was "different." In her teen years, her parents became aware of her sexual orientation and her mother could never accept that aspect of her life. She did not communicate with her brother for many years, not because of her lesbianism, but also because she was with a black woman. After several years, he got to know Marcy and eventually came to respect her. She experienced emotional and physical rejection from her sister and brothers in law. Although her sister accepted her, the brother in law would not allow Marcy in their home because of their lesbian relationship. Mary missed a lifetime of closeness with her sister because she was gay and her lover was black. Family events excluded them and Mary still suffers from the feelings of rejection.

Growing up, she felt a great sense of isolation and that she was never quite "good enough" for her family or her God. She and her partner Marcy attend a gay church, because they feel accepted here, but do not have close friends with whom they socialize. She has sensed an undercurrent of racial isolation, even among her gay and lesbian family.

They have found some opportunities for socialization at the local senior center, however most of the people are heterosexual, and they are not accepted as a lesbian couple. Mary has a strong faith in God, yet struggles with past rejections and isolations.

Her early years of faith were forged in the Catholic Church, and she was not free to be known as a lesbian. She was in one relationship in those early years with a woman who had contact with a group called "the Children of God" or the "Family of Love" Moses David Berg was the founder of the group, which had a strong emphasis on free and liberating sexual experiences within the cult. Their purpose and involvement with the group was to reveal the error of the Bible teachings of their leader, and to convince the members to defect. While the teachings were intended to proclaim love, Mary and her partner did not find a loving acceptance for their relationship.

She later discovered the Metropolitan Community Church is Los Angeles and spent almost 10 years involved in the outreach to the community.

Mary describes herself as an introvert and finds it easy to fade into the background of groups, especially those where her sexual orientation is not accepted.

She earned her living for many years as a social worker, where she was "out" to her co-workers. She was also a medical worker for several years in the Pasadena area. She was in charge of staffing the office, making hospital visits and promoting their services. She was responsible for testing applicants and assigning their positions. The company eventually closed due to company financial problems.

Prior to working with Kelly Health Care, Mary was employed by the Long Beach Police Department as a Public Affairs Officer. Her job was to interact with the senior community and inspect residences for safety problems. She would install locks on doors and windows and many times just visit with the lonely people who had no contact with family or friends.

Her experience has been that guilt will keep folks from church. Because there is something different about them that would make them unacceptable in society and in Church, she and Marcy continue to experience isolation in their senior years.

Mary spent very little time in bars, although that is where much of the southern California gay community finds one another. She and her partner would go out mostly to be able to dance together, and not for the drinking. Mary shared the story of her involvement in the West Coast version of Stonewall.

In the early 1970's, there was a protest at Barney's Beanery in West Hollywood. Since the 1940's a sign had appeared on the wall that said "Fagots-Stay Out". The Beanery was not a gay club, but was a meeting place for regulars like Jim Morrison and Janis Joplin. The sign became so offensive to local homosexuals that in 1964 Life magazine did an article in opposition to the sign. It stayed until 1970 when the Gay Liberation Front organized a picket at the restaurant. Morris Kight, along with over a hundred activists, including the Rev. Troy Perry and members of the MCC were involved in the demonstration. For three days, they took over the seats at the bar and ordered coffee so they wouldn't be arrested for vagrancy. They prevented other patrons from ordering. Some of the protestors were "roughed up" by sheriff deputies but that only brought more protestors. Mary is proud of her involvement with that protest, and while not as well known as the Stonewall Riots of 1969, it was a statement that discrimination would not be tolerated on the west coast in our community.

Mary feels that being free to love and live openly as a lesbian is still a dream not realized, but not forsaken. She and Marcy are pioneers in a long term relationship, and speaking out where they can make a difference. She has chosen to live her faith quietly, and stand beside her partner for life, knowing that being a lesbian is not the most difficult issue they address.

When I asked her why she wanted to share her story with me, she responded softly but with conviction.

"I want someone to know I was here, that my life mattered."

I have found that underlying theme in almost every interview I conducted. Their lives not only matter, they are part of piecing together the story of women and their influence through every generation. One such woman who has touched the artistic world with her paintings is Shannon.

Chapter 4
The Korean War and Security Clearance

Shannon Wood (78 years young).
Plein-air Painter- California

The interview started out with a clear statement of purpose. "I just wanted to live my life without joining causes or being "out" in public"

This is the evaluation of her life, as Shannon reflects back over her years. She has been a widow over three years, after 37 years of life with her best friend Jean.

Shannon was born in Iowa and was an only child. Her mother earned a living as a chef, and her father sold real estate. Although she knew she was "different" at an early age, she never discussed her attraction to women with her parents. Everyone accepted her relationships as "girlfriends" and never brought up lesbian attractions.

Shannon always believed her relationships were a private matter, as was her faith, being brought up in the Catholic Church. Her first serious relationship was in the early 1950's and when both of them joined the Army, they knew it had to remain private. The Korean War was in full swing, and Shannon was deployed to Italy. There were many lesbians in her unit however she soon learned that speaking of her sexual orientation would lead to being dismissed from service. She kept her own council and soon had a security clearance that would benefit her long after her military commitment.

Once out of the service, she worked for several government contractors, including Hughes Aviation and Rockwell in the 80's. She had a fear of being outed and losing her job and never felt safe from exposure. Her top secret clearance was more important than making a "statement for the cause."

She recalls a time while in the army when the CID went to Eisenhower and said "We need to clear the gays out of the Army."

A well respected personal secretary was in the room and when he consulted with her, the reply was, "Well, you'll have to start with me."

Although "Don't ask-Don't tell" was not the rule, Eisenhower decided not to go on a witch-hunt and leave the matter closed. She was the best secretary of his career.

Shannon and Jean moved to Santa Monica in the early 1970s. Shannon had a deep love of art, and had gone to school at the Ringling art school in Sarasota Florida for 18 months, then to Khachini Art school in Phoenix, ending up at the university of Arizona in Tempe to study the Indian influence of Southwestern art.

Jean and Shannon eventually settled in Cambria California and opened a framing/art store where they could own their own business. They had lived for a time in the San Francisco Bay area, but found the artistic community in the south to be more to their liking.

Jean passed away a few years ago, and Shannon has been adjusting to life without her partner. The cool, foggy days of the California Coast are often reflected in her paintings. Her status as a widow is not affirmed by the society of artists with whom she associates. Many know she lost her best friend, but she is not free to share that it was more personal and intimate. Her paintings are left to reflect the solitary existence of life now lived without her partner.

It is not uncommon for older lesbian women to choose to live by themselves. Their lives are often filled with memories that have created a lifetime of expression that few can appreciate or understand. The reality of life lived is contained in bits and pieces shared with those who knew the ones who are now departed.

Such was the experience I shared in hearing Fran's story.

Chapter 5
WW II In Europe

Fran Collins- 93
Retired Nurse
Morro Bay-California

A white haired, slightly hunched over, small frame of a woman greeted me at the door. Her voice was strong and her mind was sharp. "Come in, I've been expecting you."

I stepped into her two story townhouse cluttered with many reminders of by-gone years. She had a broad smile and was ready to take charge of the interview.

I turned on my tape recorder and opened my lap-top.

Fran slowly picked up a stack of black and white photos. "I want to start at the beginning so that you will know me." The first photo she handed me was of a large family, with stair-step children. She pointed to a young girl in the middle. "This is me." She pointed to a young man in his teens. "And this is my favorite brother."

"There were nine of us children. We grew up in Holland, Michigan, which is a Dutch community. I had a fun childhood that was always one adventure after another." She paused.

"We had a boat with rails that we put a sail on and would surf across the ice in winter. I was never afraid of anything."

"This is the picture of the boat?" I reached for another precious black and white memory."

"My girlfriends and I were always doing daring things, even without my brother. We would go up to the lighthouse along Lake Michigan and climb up to the tower. We would jump off into the channel!" She laughed at herself and the fond memory.

"So, you were somewhat of a tomboy. Did you realize you were attracted to women"?

"We'll get to that a little later"! She smiled; she definitely had an agenda in telling her story. "When I was in high school, I had flaming red hair and lots of boyfriends"!

"I can see that you were a bit feisty."

Her eyes twinkled with delight. "I sure was." She paused, "I graduated from high school in 1933. That was the year of the World's fair in Chicago and I was allowed to attend with my family. The theme was *A Century of Progress* and although the nation was still recovering from the depression of 1929, the fair focused on scientific and technological progress. I wanted to be a part of the recovery, and felt inspired to go into nursing. One of my older sisters was the 2nd ever Stewardess on United Airlines, and she gave me a graduation trip to New Jersey. I had a brother who lived on Long Island, and there was a nursing school in New Jersey that he helped me get signed up to attend."

She laughed softly, more to herself as if the memories were not over 50 years old. "There was an event shortly after I enrolled, where one of the older nurses invited me to her home overnight. It was against the rules to be gone without permission, but I found her exciting, and went anyway. Of course, I got caught, and they suspended me for a month. I finally graduated and went into Emergency Room nursing. I still wasn't sure exactly what I wanted to do, so I attended the University of Michigan, and got my B.S. in public health, and I began working in the school district."

She picked out another photo of women in military uniforms. "When the war got going in the early 40's, it wasn't just the men who wanted to enlist. I felt I could do the job for my country and joined the Army-Air force, doing nursing. I wanted to go to Europe to assist the war efforts. Initially, I was sent to Patterson field in Dayton Ohio in 1943. That was the basic training area for the Army Air Force nursing units.

Instead of being sent to Europe, I was reassigned to Kelly field in San Antonio Texas, in late 1943. I received orders from Washington DC to be deployed with the overseas unit however I was cut and I was moved to Austin Texas with other nurses and assigned to work with the ground force Army. I wanted to be in the middle of the battle, and that was still in Europe. A large group of nurses had been sent to the Pacific when the US entered the war when Japan bombed Pearl Harbor. I was still determined to be where they needed my skills most and for me, that was Europe."

I sat transfixed as I listened to this story of determination and commitment to go where the battle was and do her job. It had never occurred to me before, that the nurses who served in WW II were there because they wanted to serve, just like the men!

"It was several weeks before I was able to arrange a personal interview with Col. Klobshadow who was in charge of the nursing corps. She was coming on an inspection tour. I wrote a detailed letter to explain my desire to be with the action and use my nursing skills. Within two weeks, my orders were for the European front and I was headed straight to the Omaha Beach conflict. It was mid 1944, and my unit landed first in England and then we went on a LCI landing craft across the English Channel. The water was too rough, so we had to anchor in the channel for several days. My unit had been dispatched in such a hurry that we were all still in class "A" uniforms, rather than medical garb. After 4 days we were allowed to wash our clothes. But we were still in Class A uniforms when we were put on the troop ship."

She chuckled as she recalled that at one point they were on a troop ship and had to go down the rope ladder to board a landing barge. They were to be assigned to a field hospital, but spent their first days in a deep trench that had been created by the ground forces. Fran had an area map and was able to find an engineering unit. They went there, and were supplied with better rations than the K-rations of the field troops.

By this time, Fran had risen to the rank of First Lieutenant, and had charge of many nurses working the battlefield Quonset hut. The operating room was under her direction. They were the 189th general hospital and one of the closest field hospitals to the German lines. They were located near an airfield, so that casualties could be airlifted in for care. That winter was a hardship because of the weather and the casualties. In the spring they broke camp and followed the 101st airborne unit deeper into France.

The demands of patching up the wounded soldiers didn't leave much time to think about dating, but Fran had a close relationship with a male doctor named Ray Botto. When they did have free time, they would group date with others in their unit. She cared deeply for Ray. At that point of her life, she didn't give any consideration to the idea that she had an attraction for women.

She recalled that first Christmas in Europe. They found a small catholic church and decided to attend midnight mass. Enemy paratroopers were dropping everywhere in the countryside, but they decided to go out in spite of the danger. The priest was delighted to see Americans, and even more delighted when they all decided to drop American dollars into the collection plate. There was no place else to spend their money.

Ray was a 101st Airborne Paratrooper and had been assigned to a unit where he was in contact with General Eisenhower. Soon, excitement began to build about a meeting that would end the European conflict. Ray discovered that Lt.Gen.Walter Bedell Smith, who was Eisenhower's chief of staff, was to meet at Eisenhower's headquarters in the little red schoolhouse just inside the French border. He met with Gen.Col.Alfred Gustav Jodl, who was Germany's chief of operations staff. He was the only person authorized by the post Hitler government to make the unconditional surrender. It was May 7, 1945. Eisenhower was not at the surrender ceremony itself, refusing to attend because Jodl was not of equal rank, and Eisenhower feared he would seize the access to issue new demands. Instead, Ike came down minutes after the signing for the famous photo of him making a V for victory with the pens used for the ceremony. He later went on to become the 34th president of the United States while Gen. Jodl was hanged in Nuremberg in 1946 for war crimes.

Fran had only a vague understanding of these historic events as her unit continued to patch up the wounded and prepare them for return to the states. Their field hospital was the staging area for all the units as they were shipped out to different locations. As the healthy men were being reassigned, they had to qualify in parachute jumping, before being shipped out.

Ray was one of the men up for reassignment and during his practice jump, the lines became tangled and he was killed upon impact.

It was not the first loss of life she experienced, or the last, but Ray's death was a great loss. She spent a few more months in France, hearing of the concentration camps and the physical condition of those who were rescued. Fran returned to the States in 1945.

She still wanted to pursue nursing, and remained committed to that profession for many years. She recalls her first experience of being with a woman; it was her relationship with Edna Schrik, M.D. They had been childhood friends and over the years had lost contact. Edna was not monogamous, although their friendship continued until Edna's death in the 1970's from Alzheimer's. They did not live together for many of those years but shared a mutual interest in golf until Edna found a new love interest and moved to Hawaii.

Fran was pensive. She had a faraway look in her eyes. "I was honored to receive an invitation to the funeral service when the president died."

I interjected. "Which president was that?"

She looked and me and shook her head. "Roosevelt, of course"!

I realized that her history was of an earlier generation than mine.

She ended the interview with these comments. "No one ever knew I was gay. I didn't share it with my family, and it had to be a secret in the military. I've not had a relationship with anyone in over 30 years, but I have many good friends."

She gazed at the photos taken during that war so removed from my memories, and muttered, "Our times were the best of times."

Chapter 6
Walking With Mlk

Betty Mae Edmundson-88 years young.
Retired Social Worker
Los Osos, California

It was well after dark as we drove to keep an interview appointment with Betty Edmundson. The small coastal town of Los Osos was minutes away from Morro Bay, and seemed worlds away from a thriving lesbian community. Betty was just one of many older women who had agreed to share their history with me.

I found their home and walked to the door. I was met by Rachel and introduced myself as the journalist who was documenting stories of older lesbians. She took me to the front room and introduced me to her spouse, a white haired woman with a broad smile.

"Thank you for agreeing to meet with me." I said as I quickly set up my laptop. I handed them each a release form and list of proposed questions.

Rachel read them over. "What kind of book is this?" She sounded concerned about why I was gathering information."

"I'm doing interviews with lesbians who are willing to share stories. I want to show how we have been involved with all aspects of life for many years." I paused. "I know there have been other books written along these lines, but I want to collect snapshots of women who may not otherwise have a voice."

"That sounds alright with me," Betty spoke softly. "I don't think I'm really unusual." She began to share her early life story.

"I knew I was attracted to girls in grade school. I didn't do anything about it back then. I would sleep over at my girlfriend's homes and we would talk and giggle all night. I met Ross, my first husband, in high school. We were married when I was eighteen. The war was on, and Ross was killed in action a week before it was over. I had a young son, so I moved in with my mother and raised him with her help. I received my husband's GI benefits and went to UCLA. I majored in history, and did my student teaching at a junior high in Los Angeles."

She continued, "I started working at the Rand Corporation in research and development. It was there that I met Ed, who later became my second husband. It was the early 50's, and working for a government non-profit organization was a highly desired job. I was in Santa Monica in their aircraft division helping with statistics that required a top secret security clearance. I worked for them until 1963."

"During those early years, I felt I should return to school and get my masters degree. I met a woman named Pat at work, and we became very close. My son, Steven, was not getting along with Ed, his step-father, and that put a strain on our family relationships. Pat suggested that Steven and I move in with her. It seemed just as easy to have a relationship with a woman as it had with men, and we became lovers for a couple of years. Eventually, I began to feel smothered, as Pat was a very controlling person. I moved to a separate residence and began dating men again."

She took a deep breath. "I took a job as a social worker in Los Angeles while I worked on my masters. I was still attracted to women, and soon met Rosie who worked at NASA. We had a short lived relationship, and I lived in Laguna during that time. It was the 60's and the attitude of society was beginning to change, but I was still fairly closeted when it came to sharing my life with my family.

I took a job, training other community workers on mental health issues. We would become involved in different neighborhoods. I met a woman named Carol, who had similar interests and we lived together for two years. My life had been pretty involved with raising my son, and getting an education, and doing whatever work I could to support those goals. Relationships were stressed and after two years, I decided to buy a home in West L.A. and live alone."

Betty chuckled and looked at Rachel. "That didn't last long. Rachel and I got together in 1971, and we have been together ever since then."

Rachel interjected. "It just took her awhile to find the right person."

"I couldn't keep breaking in new lovers!" They moved to Seal Beach and Betty commuted to Long Beach to work with family services for the next ten years."

She paused for a long moment. "I was more comfortable with my homosexual relationships when it came right down to it. It was a right fit. I never discussed our life with my family, we were doing 'don't ask –don't tell" long before the military adopted that motto.

"Have you ever experienced violence because you are a lesbian?" I questioned.

"No. I've known some who have, but I kept a pretty low profile socially and in my employment. I don't apologize for who I am; it feels right to just be me." Her eyes lit up with the excitement of a memory. "The one time of my life when I didn't keep a low profile has been the most important thing I've ever done."

She continued. "In 1965 I joined the march from Selma to Montgomery with Martin Luther King. I believe in civil rights and justice for everyone. I was one of the few white women on that march. There were people killed and who suffered violence for being who they were, and no other reason. That march influenced my life to pursue equality for all, and I'm proud to have my name on the wall of Tolerance in Montgomery. It is a powerful statement by over

100,000 people from around the world who have pledged to fight hate and injustice."

"Wow. I've never known anyone who took part in that segment of history." I exclaimed.

"I think that in many ways we are still fighting similar battles for equality and justice. I'm proud of who I am and our life together. I don't have to go to church to have a spiritual dimension to my life. I attended church as a child, but I feel that God leads me and is part of my life as I stand for equality for all." She paused once again, and then continued. "Being a lesbian is who I am, and I want the world to know! I wouldn't change anything about my life."

I turned to Rachel, who is 72 years young and continues to work with an AIDS support network in San Luis Obispo. "What would you like to add to this interview?"

"We've both been involved in the David Kilbern History Project, and supporting the gay community in this area. We're active in the Gay and Lesbian Alliance in San Luis Obispo, me, more than Betty. We consider ourselves to be feminists and are proud of our community. I have a great deal of hope for future generations, because of the work done by our community. It's not limited to sexual orientation or gender; we have lots of friends who are male, female, straight and gay. My dream is that one day we will all be treated as equal. We're just not there yet."

Chapter 7
A UNIQUE MINISTRY

Pastor "Moe"-Age 70 +
(Involved in Prison Ministry)

It has been over 10 years since she heard and answered the call to visit those in prison and share the good news of the Gospel. Pastor Moe was at the age where she could have settled into retirement and lived out the rest of her life in leisure. God had a different plan for her life, and she has found it to be one of the most rewarding ventures of her life. "A Servant's Prison Ministry" was born and continues to shine light into the darkness of incarceration.

Moe was born in the desert town of Beaumont California. She had a twin brother, and was devastated when at the age of eight he died in a fire. She was a quiet child, and kept to herself a lot during those early years.

Moe felt that she always knew she was gay, but never talked with her family about her feelings. She was never attracted to men and thought that whatever was going on inside her was unique to her. She thought she was the only one who had these feelings and she was unclear what to do about them.

She shared about the first time she walked into a Gay Bar as a young woman and saw other women dancing. "I thought I'd died and gone to heaven." She laughed. "It was an eye opening experience, and I knew I wasn't the only one."

Moe left the desert for a larger city, and decided to attend the University of California in Berkley and obtain her degree. Education was a priority to her and she obtained a health care degree and a State of California Nursing degree. She became the first woman in California to be licensed for a board and care operation, and is proud that her license number is 003. It was always a male dominated profession. The licensing moved in stages, and initially she could have only three residents, then six and finally she was authorized to care for fifty residents.

Moe was close with her grandmother and cared for her until her death. She felt she had a special understanding with the elderly and was caring for Alzheimer's patients' years before there was the recognition and diagnosis process in effect today.

Her commitment to work didn't leave a lot of time for a social life; however she met and committed herself to Patty, her partner for 27 years. Patty was short in stature, a quality that she inherited from her mother. Patty was the daughter of the original World War II icon, "Rosie the Riveter"

Rosie was a small woman, and could get out to the end of the wings to rivet the metal on planes. In 1942 she was honored by a poster that shows a strong arm, and the words, "We can do it." across the image. Patty took her mother's determination as her own, and was active in the battle for equality for the LGBT community. She stood on the front lines of demonstrations as early as the 1970's, chaining herself with others to protest unfair proposed legislation with the Briggs Initiative. The Briggs Initiative is sometimes referred to as the birth of affirmative action; this legislation was viewed by many as unfair. It is still debated today, although the courts have upheld its legality.

In 1996 Moe became a born-again Christian and obtained a Ministerial degree from Liberty University in Lynchburg Virginia. She and Patty traveled extensively doing evangelistic work until Patty's death a few years ago. She had been sick for three years and underwent many surgical procedures, trying to find the source of her illness. After her death, Moe became resigned to the idea that she would be alone for the rest of her life. She knew that finding someone who would support her as a pastor's spouse and share her passion for prison ministry was not very likely. Once again, God had a different idea.

After several years of being a lesbian widow, a woman entered her life. Dolores was led to be her helper in ministry. Moe and Delores had their Holy Union in 2010.

Moe laughs as she says "You're never too old to find love. The thing was I just had to quit looking."

As Moe reviewed her life, she said she had never been harassed for being gay in the working world, because she was self employed. It was a non-issue. She doesn't feel roles play a major role in relationships now. When she was younger it was more of an issue for her to be the provider and care taker. She says her relationship is more equal now.

I asked what she would like the world to know about lesbians.

"We're just like everyone else. I may have been held back because of being a woman, but not because I was a lesbian." She paused. "I am the woman God created me to be, and my life is not over yet."

A note from Darlene: As we age, there is a tendency to think we have already lived the best years of our lives. The sense of being a contributing member of society is often diminished when we retire from the working world. I worked for the same company for 36 years, and my identity was tied into my job. I spent several years in quiet depression, because I didn't know who I was without the label of my company. I know that not everyone feels that isolation and depression, but many of the women I spoke with, expressed similar emotions.

I have found that keeping active, and using my time to invest into the lives of those around me, has been challenging and rewarding. I've been able to encourage the generations who follow me and speak out on issues that are making current history.

The friendships I have forged in my later years have strengthened my resolve to make a difference, whether in just one life, or on a national level. Often, I find that as I spend more time listening to the stories of others, my life is expanded as is my understanding of the importance of our presence as a lesbian community. The memories we are making today is the history that will be spoken of in the future.

Each woman has enhanced my life, as is the case with my next interview.

Chapter 8
The Power Of Choice

Jeanne De Joseph Aged 68
Retired Midwife

It seems like Jeanne's life was to be connected with the mystery of birth from the time of her own conception. Her mother had miscarried one child, and had been trying to conceive again, to no avail. Her mother had converted to her husband's Catholic faith when she married and made a novena to the Blessed Mother for a child. On the last day, Jeanne was conceived.

Born in Bridgeport Connecticut in the early 1940's, she remained an only child. Through grammar school, high school and college, she attended Catholic institutions. One of Jeanne's earliest memories includes having an altar in her bedroom on top of a small white bookcase. A statue of Mary and a small votive candle were the objects on her altar. What she prayed for is now forgotten. That she prayed daily is what she remembers.

She would often wake in the middle of the night during the summer to sit in a special chair by an open window in her room. She would rest her head on a pillow and watch the stars and the moon in the stillness, and feel the cool breeze on her face. The night sky was sacred, and that time being a part of nature was precious.

She kept daily diaries during her early years and saved them all until just before she got married. Another important childhood memory for her was about actions and their consequences. A memento remains on her forehead still today, as a "disobedience scar". Her dad had called her in from playing when she was about five years old; she didn't want to come and so ran away from him. She tripped on a stone in the back yard and fell, splitting open a gash in her head. There was lots of drama, and a trip to the emergency room. The take-away message:—Obey your parents or bad things would happen!

Jeanne enjoyed a close relationship with her father, taking walks in the woods and learning to enjoy and respect nature. To this day, it is part of her journey to walk gently on the earth. Her relationship with her family was critical to her. She told me that she was 12 years old before she realized that not everyone went to their grandmother's house after church on Sunday. Her mom, her dad, his two brothers and their wives and children would all gather after church and have breakfast together. All holidays were spent with family. Since her cousin Bob is only four months older than she, family was expanded to her school life because the cousins both attended the same schools for grammar school and high school. Even now, in their senior years, the two cousins are close and email frequently.

Jeanne says she developed an attraction for boys about age 15 when she met Bill while she was at Notre Dame high school. She began to have sex early and enjoyed having several boyfriends while excelling in school, dancing and having fun with girlfriends. She was president of her class, and in the honor society.

She worked in a labor and delivery unit at a local hospital from the age of sixteen. Although she was a ward clerk in the summer, she knew that she wanted to work in the labor and delivery department. When she saw her first baby born, she knew she would become an OB nurse.

She graduated from Boston College in 1965 with a Bachelor's degree in Nursing. Her college years were important to her unfolding intellectual understandings, as well as her spiritual perceptions. Philosophy and theology were taught along with information about the clinical practice of nursing. Jeanne's theology professor, a Jesuit priest rocked her world that first year of college when he told the class "your responsibility as young Catholics is to develop a 'right conscience" and if that leads you away from the Catholic Church, **so be it**". She remembered that statement, and reflected on it as she developed her adult spirituality. Boston is a real college town, and she continued to date boys from Boston College and other colleges in the area. She loved learning about the many different types of nursing practice, but her first love was still obstetrics.

In 1965, just before she married Bill, at age 20, she decided to use artificial birth control. This was not an acceptable practice for Catholics. That was the first rift in the practice of Catholicism. The second crack in her Catholic faith was in 1966 with the Pope's position on killing in Viet Nam. He never spoke against it, but insisted that abortion was a mortal sin because taking a life was wrong.

"Those dueling ideological positions seemed illogical to me then, and they do to this day, because I believe all life is sacred." Jeanne and Bill wanted children and after a time it became apparent that her dream of having five children was not to be.

Bill was in the military for four years, serving 13 months in Vietnam. He was an officer, and like most of the men returning from that conflict, he was changed. This was one of the first wedges in their relationship. Upon his release from the military, he went to work for a company in Connecticut. They moved to Utah, and Jeanne entered Graduate School in nursing at the University of Utah. Until that time, she had only taken short term commitments that she could leave as soon as she got pregnant. When that didn't happen, she made the commitment to attend graduate school to become a nurse-midwife with a master's degree. Jeanne and Bill lived apart during that time because where he worked was 90 miles north of where she went to school. They saw each other on weekends and holidays.

During her first year of the master's program, Jeanne became a feminist. She continued to treasure the times when she assisted families through the process of birth. She felt solid in her choices, both professional and personal. She very much enjoyed her friendships with women. It was through her friendship with another student and then seeing that woman together with her "roommate" in their apartment, that she realized they were lesbians. She understood with that revelation, that she was also a lesbian. She was coming into her own; she was already a feminist, and so becoming a lesbian was an easy "fit".

Monogamy had never been a high priority for her; being honest about her non-monogamy was not a priority either. She didn't consider herself bisexual, but a lesbian in transition even though she was still having sex with men, while beginning to have sex with women as well. She believed that at least at this point, being a lesbian was a mental commitment, not an emotional or even a necessarily physical connection.

After earning both a master's and a doctoral degree, she went to UCLA, where she was teaching undergraduates and graduate students in obstetrical nursing. Bill had been transferred to Georgia, and her concerns about moving there ended when Bill was fired. He moved out to California and joined her.

About this time, she accepted a position as an Assistant Director of Nursing for Perinatal and Pediatric Nursing at Stanford University Hospital that was offered to her by a colleague who was the Director of Nursing and a former student with her at the University of Utah.

During those years, Jeanne felt it was more central to her identity that she was a feminist than a lesbian: a belief she still holds. Women are the top priority in her friendships, and her world. When she came out as a lesbian, she didn't look back. So, after a while, she asked for and got a divorce from Bill.

It was several years after she divorced before she decided to tell her mother that she was a lesbian. The response surprised her when her mother said, "As long as you're happy, that's all that matters." Her mother paused, and then added, "I'm glad everyone else in the family is dead so I don't have to tell them!"

She did not find that same acceptance in her faith community. Because she was a lesbian, she was not welcome to participate in the church of her childhood. Many of the other Christian churches she visited have rules that have decided that who she is, and that whom she loves is a sin or mistake in creation.

Jeanne told me she has never experienced violence for being gay or discrimination in her places of employment. She feels the only discrimination she has experienced is due to being overweight, and that has been something she has dealt with all her life. She feels the best thing about being a lesbian is that she is comfortable in her skin, and is surrounded by her "own kind" There was frequently an emotional void with most men that is not often present with women. The women she has known "get it" and there is not the stress of trying to be who she is not.

Early relationships with women generally ended because the partner wanted more than Jeanne was willing or able to give. In one very important relationship, Jeanne felt invisible because the woman didn't want to be part of the lesbian community, or "out" to their friends. As a feminist, Jeanne was not one who would deny her identity. They have remained friends through the years, but Jeanne needed a partner who was an "out" lesbian with similar feminist and economic values and commitments. She found that relationship twenty eight years ago, with her partner Sue.

They met through the Cassandra Nursing Network. Sue was working on her doctorate at the time and Jeanne was attracted at least partially because of Sue's integrity as an out lesbian.

They have shared a committed, monogamous relationship for 28 years and have always been able to support each other in their careers and personal lives. Jeanne says roles are not important and she doesn't relate to the "butch/femme" stereotypical roles and practices of earlier generations. The women who came out as part of the second feminist movement of the 1970's have a different perspective on being lesbian than many younger women talk about now, at least those who publish their thoughts in Ms. Magazine! She doesn't see herself as a role model, because the next generation of women, feminists and lesbians, is so far from her experience that she can't imagine anyone looking to her for advice.

In her earlier years she was a separatist for a short time when she was first becoming a feminist. Men were "the oppressor" and she didn't want men to be part of her life. She feels she is currently "anti-patriarchy" rather than a separatist. She does have straight male friends; with some of them she is very close. But she doesn't have close gay male friends because in her experience, some seem not to value women and too often demean them. However she has some excellent gay male professional colleagues, and has enjoyed working with them. She is determined to live and share the values of feminism, as they are a central part of her identity, her commitments, and her life.

If she could change anything about her life, she would change her weight a lot sooner. With age, came a lot of health problems she could have perhaps avoided. No matter what might have been different, life is what it is. As it is so commonly said today: "You play the cards you are dealt".

Her spiritual path has been winding from Catholicism to explorations of a form of Protestantism, to Mormonism, to Quakerism and to earth-based spiritualties, especially practices of American Indians of the Plains like vision quests and teepee meetings. She has developed an adult spiritual understanding as a result of following that path, and she has chosen Paganism, more specifically Dianic Wiccan practices combined with some elements of American Indian practices for her spiritual home. This spiritual path challenges her to be the best she can be, to decide what is right and wrong for herself and to walk gently on the earth. Her spirit is cradled by the universe; all that is the earth and nature is present within her. Jeanne says that her central spiritual practice today is gratitude.

Her "temporal" path has also evolved. In addition to close ties with some members of her family of origin, she has a partner who loves her as well as friends, professional colleagues, and a family of choice who also loves her and wants to spend time with her. Although her basic education was in nursing, she has been a teacher, an administrator, a researcher, a clinical nurse and a midwife, all within the practice of nursing. She has had a full and satisfying career and is grateful for the many opportunities to learn and grow that she has experienced She is grateful for the colleagues who have enriched her life.

Jeanne is in a reflective time of her life now, considering what have been her gifts and challenges, and what legacy she would like to leave. Her story is still in process, and her life is still unfolding. She looks back with fondness and a wry appreciation for all those gifts and challenges. She lives fully in each moment with gratitude, and she looks forward with hope and excitement to the future, whatever it may bring.

Chapter 9
Vietnam

Astrid Ortega Army Nurse Corps
Santa Rosa- Nurse Practitioner
67 years young

Astrid moved from Merida Yucatan Mexico to Providence Rhode Island when she was 4 years old. They were the first Mexican family in 1949 to immigrate there, and her family was profiled in the town newspaper. She still has the article.

Her father was a physician at Roger William Hospital, and she spent many hours there watching him at work in the radiation department. At age 15, she knew she wanted to be a nurse. A couple of years later, while a student at RI hospital in providence, she heard about the Army Nurse corps that would pay your schooling if you enlisted and you could get your RN license.

When she was 20 years old, she did just that. It was 1966 and America was just at the beginning of its longest and perhaps most brutal war. Viet Nam was the furthest place from her thinking when she went to Fort Sam Houston for officer training. She wanted to be a nurse, and wanted to serve in an Army Hospital. They sent her to Letterman Army Hospital in Presidio, San Francisco. She soon discovered that she was the property of the Army, and all parts of her life were scrutinized. Her plans for a future were interrupted when in July 1967 she was given orders to ship out to Viet Nam. Astrid's objections were ignored, and on August 10ᵗʰ she left Travis Air Force base on a 24 hours flight to Tan Son Nhut Airport in Saigon. She was obligated to serve one year in Viet Nam, which would fulfill her military commitment.

Fighting in Vietnam began in 1959 and continued through 1975. American troops were not active during all those years; however the staggering death toll was over 58,000 men. It is unclear how many women, mostly nurses served their country in Viet Nam to support the troops. The estimates range from 7,500 to 11,000. One thing is clear. Eight nurses are recorded as losing their lives during that conflict.

Astrid was sent to the 36ᵗʰ Evacuation hospital in Vung Tau. It was located about 50 miles south of Saigon along the coast of the South China Sea. The area had miles of tropical beaches and plenty of sunshine. Many of the wounded GI's came to this area for R & R, and to not be reminded that a war was going on all around them. Often on their days off, the nurses would join the American and Australian soldiers on the beach. There were other sections on the beach for nationals and other Korean military. Those areas were off limits to the American nurses.

The hospital was near the small town of Vung Tau, which had 300 bars and 600 bar gals to entertain the troops. Astrid states she got a crash course about prostitution and V.D. The Vietnamese women were beautiful and mostly dressed in white gowns, and carried black umbrellas for protection from the sun. Many of the GI's found their way into the hospital, not from war wounds, but from diseases contracted from their sexual encounters.

The nurses, doctors and officers were housed in a three story building called the Villa Dubois. It was a French hotel, which was quite comfortable. Each room was a double with a shower and toilet. It was about 5 miles from the hospital itself. There was a gazebo at the building in front, which was in use around the clock, and there was no limit to the events they found to celebrate. The nurses mostly ate their meals at the officers club or other military clubs in Vung Tau. Although there were frequent mortar bombings in the area, the hospital at Vung Tau was considered to be the safest place in Vietnam.

Astrid was promoted to a 1st Lieutenant the first month she was in Vietnam. She was the assistant head nurse of a GI post-operative ward that housed more than 40 men in their late teens. Most of the patients were arm and leg wounds, and many were frequently double amputees. Astrid recalls spending "hours removing shrapnel with nothing more than tweezers. The nurse's schedule was long and demanding, working 10 to 12 hours every day. The ward was constructed from half of a Quonset hut located near the beach and next to an airfield to bring in the wounded. Each hut held about 80 beds. The only running water was in the operating room. There was one laboratory, and two shower toilet facilities. The hospital was far from sanitary, and the dirt floors were a constant reminder that they were in a jungle. This was her world for the first 6 months of duty. It was heartbreaking to just get to know the men they cared for, and then have them die from their wounds. Death was the horrible consequence of a war no one wanted to fight! Then, things got worse.

Astrid took over a ward of Vietnamese women and children who had been injured and badly burned. "This was the most difficult" she recalls. "I did a lot of crying on the inside."

"There was no way that we could learn their names, so we gave them Walt Disney character names. We called them Snow White and the seven dwarfs, Mickey, Goofy, or anything else we could think of to identify them." She continued. "What impressed me was how little pain medication they would use, and they were so thankful of any kindness."

Their burns were treated with silver nitrate that had been soaked into the gauze bandages. It was the only type of antibiotic that was available. "We were dubbed the crispy critter ward because of the severity of the napalm wounds. We only had the patients that had any chance of survival. You learned not ask questions about others that were not brought into our hospital. The Vietnam hospitals were filled to capacity." She paused for a moment to remember those scenes etched forever in her memory. "When we got them stabilized, the pilots would take them back to the jungle and drop them off. We didn't ask what would happen to them since their villages had been destroyed"

As a war nurse, Astrid was exposed daily to the misery and devastation in the lives of the men who entered her hospital ward. There was a rule of "time" to heal, and if the nurses could patch up a soldier quickly, he would be returned to combat duty. On more than one occasion, they would lose the paperwork to extend the hospitalization so that the soldier could be flown home. The paperwork would eventually be found, however the soldier would be headed stateside by that time. There were many times the nurses would sign forms that the doctors should have signed. The doctors were kept busy in the operating rooms and the *"decision making"* was left to the nurses as when to return men to the United States. The war nurses were the ones who were really in charge of the hospital. Each day was a scene of life and death, and the stress took its toll on all the nursing staff.

Astrid recalls that one of the things that disturbed her most during this time was when the "lifer" nurses required you to maintain Army etiquette. This meant even if you were rushing from patient to patient trying to save lives, you must salute, even if your hands were full of blood and bandages. They insisted you wear the ugly army baseball caps because it was army regulations! The most absurd thing was insisting you not date enlisted men! It was hard to comprehend that rules were more important than lives, and given the war situation, you might not be alive the next day!

She remembers that while the hospital never came under enemy fire while she was there, that one of our own did fire upon the compound. This was because the ward was filled with local prostitutes, one of whom had given him a venereal disease.

The threat of attack did more damage to the minds of the nurses than being under physical attack from the gun fire. You never knew when or if that attack would come.

One of the things many of the nurses did to stay positive and be a bit more feminine in that military environment, was to mail order bright colored, lacy underwear. It wasn't Army issue, but it made them feel good about themselves. It was about the only personal items that the nurse's hand -washed, in order to keep them in good condition. They all had local women assigned to clean their rooms and do their military laundry. They paid $5.00 a month for the service.

When Astrid was at the end of her deployment she came up with a plan. Usually, the women would hang their underwear on the balcony. They would be reprimanded by one particular Captain who insisted on following the regulations and would yell at them to remove the clothing from view. On the day Astrid was returning to the states, she took her colorful, lacy underwear and stapled it onto the line in full view of the base. They were on the second floor, and her roommate said, "What do I do when the Captain yells for me to take it down?"

Astrid chuckled. "Tell her to come up and take it down herself. It's not yours." It was her farewell to Vietnam! She was going home.

Whatever she remembered "home" to be, this was not what she was expecting. It was August 15, 1968 when she landed at Travis Air Force Base. There were no waving flags, no crowds to welcome home the troops, nothing to say "welcome home", or "thanks for your service." Astrid was transported to Oakland Military Base to be discharged. She was handed her papers and her last check. No ceremony like when she enlisted. She had to call a friend to come pick her up because she had no cash. This was just the beginning of the lack of support she would experience as a Vietnam veteran.

The attitudes of society were strongly against the war. Astrid had lots of emotional confusion. She would be talking with people and they would say things like: "You were a fool to go to Vietnam." It didn't take too long before she stopped telling anyone she was a veteran. She had two nursing school buddies who were her emotional sounding boards. The images of war causalities were never far from her mind, and hearing planes or helicopters would often bring back those fears of attacks or being faced with burned and mangled bodies.

Astrid decided to return to New Jersey to be closer to her family. She had 2 former classmates who had also served in Tuy Hoa. They would get together on weekends and talk about their experiences. This was her first experience of a support group, and the beginning of dealing with Post Traumatic Stress Disorder. It helped to minimize the trauma because she could verbalize her fears and memories of the horror that being an Army nurse in that environment had created. If she had come home missing a limb, she would have been given treatment at the V.A. Hospital. However, gaining acknowledgment of the crippling damage done to her mind and emotions would be a long uphill battle. Compensation would be a long time coming to her and other veterans. Although many had come home...part of them was still in the jungles of Vietnam. The men didn't have support groups, and all too often could not share even with their families what they had experienced.

Astrid says that she often had bad dreams of all the horrors she had endured. The "lifer" nurses seemed to suffer even more, because as the war progressed, so did the causalities. She did go through counseling at the veteran's center, and was officially diagnosed with PTSD.

For Astrid, coming home took a long time. She had a lot of guilt about things she couldn't control, like not learning the hundreds of names of the children. Part of her healing came as she would give lectures on Vietnamese culture and worked to educate her peers in the nursing field. She feels that by sharing her knowledge with others, it helped to redeem that year in Vietnam.

Along her journey to healing, Astrid also moved back to San Jose, California and came out as a lesbian. She had not acted on her feelings while being in the Army, but as a civilian she had more freedom. She has been with her partner

Gordie for 28 years. They were part of a PBS documentary called "Freedom to Marry" several years ago. Astrid continues to educate and work for justice in the nursing field, and in the gay community. In 2008, Astrid and Gordie were legally married in the short window of time that same sex marriage was allowed in California.

Chapter 10
Murder in the work Place

Karen Mackey-67
Mountain View, California

February 16, 1988 started just as every day did for
Karen. She arrived for work in building M5 on the second
floor at ESL in Sunnyvale California. She was a Senior Staff
engineer and Section Manager in the Software Directorate.
Before that day would end, she would be part of the most
notorious mass murder in California History.

It was midafternoon when Richard Wade Farley went
on a shooting rampage that killed seven, and wounded four.
Before we look at what happened, it would be good to examine why it happened at all.

Richard Farley had worked for ESL (Electromagnetic
Systems Lab) but had been fired in 1986. He still carried
strong feelings for his former co-worker, Laura Black. He
had been harassing her since they worked together, and she
continued to spurn his advances. In a desperate move to
keep him away from her, she had filed a restraining order
against him. It was scheduled to be heard in court on February 17th, 1988.

On February 8th, Farley had followed Black to an early morning class she was taking at Santa Clara University. He placed a bizarre love note on her car. When that was ignored, he plotted to get back at her. He told investigators that he had only planned to damage some of ESL's computer equipment when he entered Building M5 on the six-building campus at 3 p.m. The carnage tells a different story.

Farley killed his first victim with a shotgun blast outside the building. He went to the north side of the building that was secured with an electronic card-key lock. He fired a shotgun blast through a door window and entered the building.

His second victim was a man sitting behind a desk immediately inside the entrance. He moved up a stairwell leading to the second floor and killed a third man with another shotgun blast to the chest.

Once at the second floor door, he shot the locking mechanism. His fourth victim was a man sitting at a desk just inside the door. He continued down the hallway shooting two more men, and two women at random.

Laura Black was among the injured, suffering a gunshot wound in the shoulder after she slammed a door in Farley's face. Farley continued his rampage down the hallways, shooting into the offices and destroying numerous computer monitors.

Twenty six employees survived the onslaught by hiding behind locked doors, under desks and even crawling into the false ceiling above the offices to escape the gunman. It was learned later in the day that Farley had armed himself with a 9mm. Browning automatic, a .30-80 caliber semiautomatic handgun, a shotgun and a high-powered rifle before going to ESL.

One of those employees was Karen Mackey. Her office was just around the corner from Laura Black. She heard loud bangs that she assumed were a noisy and sloppy delivery of equipment that was dropping onto the hallway. She walked to her doorway to see what the commotion was, when she saw a man bouncing on the floor then flip over. She saw smoke in the air, and was trying to make sense of it. At first, she thought he had fallen from the fake ceiling. A female co-worker came out of her office, and stepped over the man, asking him what was wrong. "I was just about to run down the hall and help her, when I saw guns come up and blow her away! I remember multiple guns and thought there had to be more than one person doing the shooting." She recalls, "I stepped back into my office, turned off the lights. I hid under my office-mates desk. I heard footsteps, and doors slamming, then more shots."

Karen held her breath, waiting for a shot to be fired into her office. What seemed like an eternity passed before his steps went on down the hall.

In the minutes that followed her mind raced with scenarios about who could be shooting up the place. "I thought it was terrorists that didn't like ESL's work, so they were going from room to room shooting people." My next thought was, "I have to make peace with myself, since I'm going to die very soon."

She remembers dwelling on that concept, but then another thought flashed through her mind. *Who will feed my dogs if I die?*

"I could tell that the footfalls and the shots were moving in the opposite direction, so I got up and peeked out the door."

Everything was black and white, no blood. She ran in the opposite direction. When she reached the intersecting hallway, she slowed and peeked down the corridor. Her heart was pounding with fear as she saw a gunman with multiple weapons and a double bandoleer of bullets.

"Almost at the same time, he saw me and picked up a gun and fired in my direction. I was already moving away from him and somehow missed getting shot."

She recalls running around the corner and trying to get into a combination locked room to hide inside a refrigerator, however the lock jammed. She tried again, but decided to move somewhere else when she heard footsteps slogging around the corner.

Karen paused. "I ran into an adjacent drafting room and told the guy working in there. 'There are terrorists here shooting people.

He replied. "They're not terrorists. I know exactly who it is."

"At that point, I got extreme heebie jeebies and ran out the opposite door and down the multi angled hallway to the front stairwell. I bolted out the front door and ran toward the parked cars. I was crouching behind cars, yelling to people to get down. It was a few minutes later that the police drove up."

Reports verified this entire episode of terror had lasted about 20 minutes at the point she had escaped to the parking lot. The 911 system was not in wide usage at that time, especially in enterprise phone systems. Karen was relieved that someone had called the police however she was not yet aware of the number of dead, or the negotiations that were underway to capture Farley.

Everyone who was on the company campus was evacuated to building M-1, that was well out of rifle range. No one was allowed to leave, for their own safety. Karen recalls, "I was pacing back and forth, waiting for some news that would allow us to leave. Then, I decided to call my friend Katy. She was part of a group from the El Camino Reelers, a square dance group that was to meet at my house that evening. It soon became evident that I was not going to be allowed to leave anytime soon. I also remembered that my car was in the shooting zone.

"I wasn't thinking clearly but I wanted Katy to know what was happening, and to tell the others that I would not be home in time for the meeting.

In all the chaos, it hadn't occurred to me that I was in no state of mind to meet with anyone! We were kept in M-1 for the duration of the negotiations with Farley, who was eventually wooed out of Building M-5 about 12 or 1 AM."

Meanwhile:

It was just after 7 p.m. when Farley told police they could come in for 20 minutes to remove the wounded and deceased. He began to express remorse about shooting Black, but was not at all remorseful about shooting the others.

He eventually surrendered just after midnight with the promise of a soft drink and a turkey-ham and cheese sandwich from Togos. He told the arresting officer, "I'm not crazy; I know I will die as a result of this."

It was over an hour later that the police knew the exact number of dead and injured employees. Employees, who were still in the building, told everyone that the scene was a "bloodbath". As news spread about the massacre, relatives of the ESL workers jammed phone lines trying to reach loved ones.

Farley was booked into Santa Clara County Jail for investigation of seven counts and murder and four counts of attempted murder. Black was rushed into surgery at Stanford University Medical Center with massive wounds to her left shoulder, and a broken arm. The doctor said bullet fragments traveled into her chest and that night, she underwent surgery for a collapsed lung.

The employees, who were being held in Building M-1, were finally released and allowed to go home.

Karen doesn't recall how she got home that night. Someone had to take her because her car was still in the area where the police were collecting evidence. Her friend Katy came over and spent many hours that night 'talking her down'.

Those physical wounds would heal over time for Laura Black and the others who were wounded, but for Karen Mackey and several others, the memory of that day is never far in the background of their thoughts.

The company provided individual and group counseling to help with the healing process. It was weeks before everyone returned to work, and a longer time before building M-5 was repaired from all the damage.

In 1992, Farley was sentenced to die for the murders and attempted murders. Karen was one of the many who testified at his trial, along with Laura Black. The ESL Company was acquired by another company, and the M-5 building was eventually torn down.

Karen shares that she still stays in touch with some of her co-workers and will get together with them to remember their brush with death. She left ESL in 1994 and had short job history with Lotus and Lockheed Martin. She eventually joined Cisco in 1999, until her recent retirement.

There were several good things that came from Richard Farley's conviction.

* California passed the first anti-stalking laws in the nation
* In 1993, a made for TV movie, "I can Make you Love Me" was produced with Brooke Shields and Richard Thomas.
* In 2009 the California Supreme Court upheld Farley's death sentence.

In 1996, Karen began a relationship with her now legal spouse, Nancy. Nancy has been a key element on the journey to emotional healing and health.

The anniversary date brings a flood of memories; loud noises or cars backfiring can bring instant tension and fear. There is anger and resentment that a man who killed 7 people and tried to kill 4 others just to blame Laura Black for rejecting him. He still maintains that she made him do it. He still sits on death row being supported by our taxes. Farley continues to file appeals, and cost the judicial system tax dollars. Karen states. "I resent the hell out of the fact that tax payers are footing the bill for his upkeep and appeals. Keeping him alive is a drain."

My last question for Karen: "How long before you felt safe?"

Her response: "Still waiting."

Chapter 11
The Cypress Structure

Cathi Scarpa- Grass Valley California
Semi-Retired Nurse/Artist.

October 17, 1989 started out like many of the days before. Cathi was a nurse at the University of California San Francisco Medical Center and lived "across the bay" in Alameda with Kay, her partner of 10 years.

UCSF had a Vanpool which left and returned daily between Alameda to the University. On "clinical" days, which were patient care focused, She could work at least 12 hours but had no control or advance notice of situational occurrences on those days, so would drive herself rather than rely on the schedule of the Vanpool.

Administrative Days were focused on meetings or classes, and were better suited to take the vanpool. October 17th, 1989 was one of those days.

"The night before, I had intended to drive myself into the city and set my alarm clock accordingly. However, the next morning when the alarm sounded, I briefly rethought that particular evening's traffic and the benefits of the carpool lanes. The city of San Francisco was hosting the World Series at Candlestick Park and both bay area teams were competing in the *"Battle of the Bay"*. I reset the alarm clock for an additional 30 minutes of sleep and decided to take the Vanpool. That seemingly insignificant decision was one of the choices that would change our lives forever.

Our "vanpool" group was very congenial and some were close friends. We often spoke about our families, pregnancies, temperature charts for conception, work and possible retirement options. There were times some of us would meet for coffee on the weekends. On other occasions, a few of us gathered for 'adjustment" hour and hors drovers at a local pub on Fridays.

At the end of this particular work day, the seven of us boarded the van and prepared for the trip home. I was seated in the "shotgun" position. We excitedly conversed about the World Series. One woman was wearing earrings that displayed the "San Francisco Giants" on one ear and "Oakland A's" on the other.

We had options for routes to exit the city and arrive on the Bay Bridge. The "upper route" was a freeway approach and if clear, was the quicker route. However, if heavily trafficked, there was no getting off and we would have to endure bumper to bumper all the way to the bridge.

The lower route was on surface streets through the downtown, and brought us to the last onramp to the bridge. As usual, we lightheartedly debated alternatives. Although the "upper route" appeared to be clear, no one knew what was beyond the bend so, we opted for the "street route" through the downtown to the last on ramp for the bridge. This seemingly insignificant decision, in hindsight took us at least 5 minutes longer to navigate our way to the bridge.

Just after 5:00pm we exited the bridge on to the Cypress structure. This double decker freeway had our South bound traffic on the top deck.

Within minutes, the van began to veer and we were being pulled into the lane next to our lane, as if we had a flat tire. The driver was struggling with the wheel and stated she was having a hard time correcting our direction. I took hold of the right side of the steering wheel while looking in the right side view mirror to be sure the lane was clear and attempted to assist in righting our vehicle.

After directing the vehicle into the far right lane – I looked forward and saw a "tidal wave" of concrete rising up ahead of us. As the van's forward movement propelled us up this "wave" of roadway, I remember calling out, *"Hold on everyone, we're in for a ride."*

We were propelled over the top of that *"rise"* into the unknown. The roadway beyond had collapsed, so our van sailed across in midair – crashing in to the remaining segment of standing roadway at least 30 feet ahead. We plunged down, landing upright 30 feet below. Ultimately, it was both a horizontal and a vertical crash.

I must have lost consciousness, for when I *"awoke"*, I was very sore and *"remembered"* feeling as though my body had been tumbled in a washing machine. I specifically remember thinking *this must be what Jerry Rice feels like on a Monday*. He was the highly skilled wide receiver for the San Francisco 49'ers at the time, and took a lot of hits. The thoughts that go through your brain seem odd when you are in shock.

Then, I began to wonder, – *"Am I alive or am I dead?"* All I noticed were the smells of smoke, burning rubber, gasoline and the sight of flames. It was like a scene depicting an inferno from Hell. I thought, *wow, my belief system was wrong – there is a Hell and I am there!*

Then I noticed some "earthly" billboards and realized I was in fact alive and still on earth. The bit of the freeway that was visible to me looked like a mangled mess. I saw twisted rebar hanging in weird shapes, and the crumpled remains of something protruding out of nowhere.

My chest was pinned against the dashboard and my head was outside the windshield. My legs had gone through the firewall and were in the engine compartment.

I could tell the driver was seriously injured, as her head had a gash from the steering column. I saw evidence of stomach contents on the floorboards and began hearing some soft moans from the back of the van. I began calling out to the others but received no responses. I found some small pieces of concrete that were on my chest/lap and tossed them in an attempt to waken the others. That's when I saw the muscles in my right arm exposed and bleeding.

I became aware of voices and a man from the neighborhood had climbed on this demolished unstable structure and began to comfort me. I could only see his brown plaid shirt. I asked him was it an explosion? He said no it was an earthquake! Another man came and looked inside the van and said – "This looks like a scene in a wax museum". No one was moving. All the women were still seated, heads down or to the sides – and apparently only a small amount of blood trickling from a woman's ear.

With all the fire, spilled gasoline and smoke, all I could think now was *turn the engine key off*. Whatever we had just survived, I did not want to burn to death! I could not reach the ignition key. I then began to feel a tremendous amount of heat on my legs in the engine compartment.

Another civilian rescuer arrived, as I pleaded "turn off the ignition." I tried to remain calm as I instructed him "Please get the fire extinguisher from behind the driver's seat and shoot it on the engine"

The man didn't seem to pay attention to my requests, so I reached up and grabbed his shirt. I repeated the appeal with an insistent voice and he responded. I immediately felt my legs get cool once the fire extinguisher contents reached the engine. I had no idea of the severity of my injuries.

These civilian angels were going to attempt to extricate us from the van. Since our doors were up against the right wall of the freeway, they were going to endeavor getting us out through the side window. I had limited viewing, but I heard the quiet, "no pulse" as others were being removed from the van. I thought – *that can't be true her pulse is just hard to find in this emergency situation.*

At least three of my co-workers were removed from the van before the men could pull me through between the two front seats .They would have to lift me out through the left side window. When they began to remove me from the van I said "I'm not petite" so make sure you have help. It will take at least two of you.

"How much to you weigh?" He asked.

I said, "I'm not going to tell you that" I just don't want you to hurt yourself."

I remember that first man in the brown plaid shirt staying with me even when I was on the tarmac. The "official first responders" finally arrived i.e.: Firefighters/paramedics. They began to assess my injuries. One of them took penny scissors and began cutting my pant legs and my shirt so he could better evaluate my injuries. I was now exposed for the entire world to see. Circling above were news and rescue helicopters. The man with the brown shirt took it off and spread it across me to provide a little privacy.

While they were appraising my situation I raised my head and looked at my lower extremities.

That is when I saw the bottom of my right foot facing me – "oh my" – that doesn't look good at all!" – The paramedic stated – "you're right". It seemed surreal and I had never seen anything like that in all my years of nursing. My training as a nurse helped me stay calm; however my body was in shock. I was becoming lightheaded – as now that my body was no longer *"pinned"* and I was not in a bent position.

Another man just happened to be an off duty paramedic and was able to brake right before the freeway damage. He came by, and asked if there was something he could do for me. I asked if they had some oxygen – and sure enough – he proceeded to place a mask on me – I mean – really – what are the chances!

A while later, the man in the plaid shirt inquired if I needed anything. I asked if he could go to the van and get my brief case and some money so he could call Kay and let her know I was all right.

I had no idea the extent of the damage from the quake and that all phone service was down. But he climbed down and walked for 3 blocks trying to find a working phone. He was unable to call her, but he came back to let me know, and returned my quarter! I will never forget the true heroism of these local neighbors and with no experience, who literally risked their lives, climbing up on this gnarled freeway to help complete strangers in need. They are true heroes.

They continued their work tirelessly and persisted through all the aftershocks. They were true blessings.

Over an hour had passed and during that time, I could hear from the *"walkie talkies"* that they didn't want the helicopters to land. The remaining freeway structure was unstable and even the wind from the blades were causing some movement.

I was placed on a backboard and lowered over the side to the sidewalk below. There they transferred me into an ambulance and directed the driver to *"Take her to Eden"*. I had never heard of *"Eden"*, and knew from my Trauma/ER experiences, it was possible that I was going to a holding area for comfort and not for treatment. During disaster situations, Triage makes every effort to treat the most severely injured people. By now I knew I had significant injuries that would require a lot of resources. I didn't know at the time that Eden had one of the best trauma centers in the area.

I remember being in the ambulance. It seemed that we were careening down dark streets. There was no power and it felt like we were off road because of the earthquake debris.

In the ER, my injuries were assessed. I was awake all of this time. The tibias, fibulas, feet and ankles were broken in both legs. However my right leg was more severe as my ankle had been totally broken and turned around.

Another miracle happened in that ER when an orthopedic surgeon who was off duty showed up to see if he could help with any injuries. He had been stationed in Viet Nam and had experience with major trauma cases.

Doctors on both sides of my body grasped my legs to straighten them out and help restore the circulation. The pain was so intense I yelled and flailed my arms, hitting the nurse that was standing near my head.

Later I was referred to as *"the screamer"*. At the same time, another physician had inserted a needle/tube into my abdomen, checking for blood – which would indicate internal bleeding. He found it.

I knew that was not good. The one surgeon stated if they could get me into the Operating Room there was a chance to save my legs, but it had to be done quickly. I heard, "If she lives she will never walk again." As providence would have it, because there were not many other patients who were coming into Eden for treatment, they freed up an operating room for my *"complicated"* surgery.

As they were wheeling me to surgery, I had asked if someone could again attempt to call Kay, and at least let her know where I was in the hospital.

I reached out to a nurse as they were taking me to surgery. "If there is any problem in surgery and I'm not going to have a good quality of life, please just let me go."

She tried to assure me, *"Honey, you'll be ok. Don't worry. You are in good hands."*

When the anesthesiologist came I told him the same thing. *"Listen to me...If I'm not going to come out of this with a good quality of life, just let me go."*

He spoke with assurance, *"You'll be ok"*

I began to regret that Kay and I had not completed filling out the power of attorney for health care and advance directive. *How important is it right now? Kay doesn't even know that I am here."*

Kay's story:

"I was the manager in a business park on an island in Alameda. We were across the bay from San Francisco. When the earthquake hit I was just leaving work. The buildings were shaking and people were running to find cover. I saw a co-worker struggling to keep her balance while she attempted to make her way down the hallway. I picked her up and carried her to a desk which we dove under for safety. After assessing that everyone was OK at work, I knew I needed to make my way home and check on the dogs.

I needed to find out if our home had been damaged and make sure both dogs were safe. Cathi and I had talked about what to do if there was ever a disaster, as vets would not be able to handle all the needs. We lived in a little 1920's Craftsman home, and my concern grew as I drove past rippled sidewalks and saw all the damage. Thankfully, our dogs were fine and I noted that our *"emergency evacuation kit"* on wheels was accessible. It contained all we would need in a situation like this: a tent, water, dog food, canned goods and camping supplies.

I didn't know how extensive the quake was or the extent of the damage across the Bay Area. The power was out in our neighborhood, and television service was cut off. I sat out on my porch and turned the car radio to news reports. All the local stations were not available so I was listening to one from the central valley.

I proceeded to go up and down the block helping neighbors turn off their gas mains, in case there was damage to the pipes. I knew even an accidental spark could cause a fire or an explosion.

One by one everyone returned home from their workplace and several of our neighbors came over and sat on our porch. We gathered in groups on the sidewalk, attempting to get information about the earthquake. Since we still had no power, I found a battery operated radio to listen for earthquake updates.

I wasn't concerned about Cathi, because I knew that she would go the nearest hospital to help out in a disaster. I poured a glass of wine and spent the evening with neighbors. There was minor damage to our home but nothing that needed immediate attention.

After several glasses of wine, I went to bed. About 10:00 P.M. I did get a phone call, telling me that Cathi was in the hospital in Castro Valley and I needed to get there. I didn't even know where Eden Hospital was, and I knew that with all the lights out that I had had too much to drink to be able to drive myself. I woke up a neighbor who agreed to take me to the hospital.

I walked into the emergency room, and was "signed" in. I drank coffee and waited for hours as Cathi was still in surgery. Finally the orthopedic surgeon who had been working on Cathi came out to speak with me. *"Are you her sister?"* he asked.

"No," I responded, uncertain as to what I should say. This was pre-domestic partner laws, and I knew they could keep me from seeing her.

"Are you a relative?" He asked again.

"No, I'm her partner. Do you have a problem with that?"

"I don't," he replied, *"But it will go easier if you say you are her sister."*

I agreed and he began a rundown of her injuries. Things like *"If she lives, she may never walk again. It will be six weeks before we know if we can save her legs."*.

My mind was spinning, but not from the wine. I was in shock. *How could this be happening"?*

Cathi's Injuries

"I was in surgery over 8 hours, with three surgical teams working at the same time. Two of the teams were working to repair my legs with rods, nuts, bolts and screws. The third team was repairing my lacerated liver and suturing my arm. It would be a few more weeks before anyone realized I had also broken both wrists. This first day of trauma was just the beginning of our life being turned upside down like the freeway!

I think it was the next day when I was awake and realized I was in the ICU. I began to wonder about our dogs and if they were ok. Kay had arrived and assured me they were fine, but I wasn't convinced and thought they had to be put down and that Kay didn't want to tell me the truth.

Long before this, we had a substantial portable disaster kit and a plan in place. One component of the plan was that if anything major happened and the dogs were severely injured and there were not veterinary services available, we would put them down. The only thing that convinced me our four legged pals were ok was a few days later she brought them to the hospital, and I was wheeled to a window where I could see them outside.

As the days passed, I was covered with more bruises. My chest was black from the force of the impact when the van landed. My breasts were incredibly effective airbags; however, those injuries are believed to have led to a breast cancer diagnosis years later. I had metal rods and bolts like little erector sets, holding my legs together.

Kay and I started having conversations about the impending medical bills. We could sell everything we had, and just start over. As a nurse, I knew a lot about how quickly bills would add up, and already in this short time I knew we were well beyond our means.

At that time, my only reference for how bad things were from the earthquake was my memory of the twisted rebar, crumpled concrete and collapsed roadway. It was later, I learned that 5 of the women in our van had died, and it would be weeks before I would discover that the 7.1 quake had killed 63 people across the bay area, and 42 people had perished on the Cypress structure.

I later learned that our van and fallen on a vehicle from the north-bound lane. The lady in that vehicle was discovered several hours later, as her car was under concrete and our van. *Did she live?* Years later I had the good fortune of meeting her. She said "Wow, it's great to finally meet the one who was on top!"

After some extended period of time, the University had a memorial service for the 5 people who died in the van. Although I was unable to attend any of the funerals or the memorial service, they did provide me with a tape of the service. It has helped a bit to put a sense of closure on this tragedy.

The road to recovery was months of surgeries; and physical therapy. It was quite a process to get my physical condition back to normal. I went through over twenty surgeries and bone grafts. It would be 2 ½ years before I would walk unassisted."

Kay's story

"About 6 a.m. the morning after the earthquake, the phone rang and a voice said it was *"Western Union."* They said they wanted to verify that a money transfer was legitimate, as there was some discrepancy in the I.D.

"No way! She is in intensive care due to injuries from the earthquake. Cancel that card...Don't let anyone use it!" I suddenly realized that her purse and brief case had been taken on the day of the accident! A close friend helped me go through all Cathi's papers and cancel the accounts. We were fortunate that the banks and credit card companies would perform these tasks on my say so, as we had not completed the Power of Attorney forms for such situations.

We began to hear stories about people who had gone up onto the structure, not just to assist in recovery, but some of the *"helpers"* were stealing purses and wallets and taking jewelry from bodies. One of the women in the van had her wedding ring taken off her finger while she was laid out on the freeway after being pronounced dead. I could not comprehend the callous hearts that would take advantage of this situation. It was a season of heroes and criminals.

We also had an emergency plan with some of the others on the vanpool that should something arise and we couldn't get back across the bridge that we would look out for each other's pets until everyone was home. I went to one friends home and her sister had arrived from Denver and the dog was being well cared for. I went to a second home where our friend was also a passenger on the van with Cathi. I found her family gathered there planning a memorial service. She was one of the 5 who had died that day on the structure. Up until that moment I had no idea that people in the van had died. I left and went back home with tears in my eyes and a giant ache in my heart. I was in shock.

I didn't realize how much in shock I was in that first week. I went from the hospital to home, not even thinking about work. I was cancelling credit cards, banking accounts and changing the locks on our home. I was still attempting to let friends and family know what had happened. After a week, I was sitting on the porch when my boss drove up. I had never even called into work, or thought about going to work! I told her I would be in the next week. I realized later that I hadn't even been eating!"

Cathi's journey to "normal"

"The word normal is relative. What is normal today may not be tomorrow.

As the weeks ran into months, I had a lot of time to reflect on my life, and Kay and I together, as a couple. We were in our 30's and although we talked about what we would do if something happened to us, we never got around to completing an advance directive, or durable power of attorney for health care.

She didn't think she would be able to act as my agent as she had no medical background and was unsure if she could make an informed decision in an emergency situation. She has since learned that you can take some time to make decisions and request for consultations or second opinions. Whatever your age, DO NOT PUT IT OFF! Make sure the person you appoint to make decisions for you, will follow through with YOUR WISHES."

As time went on, Cathi discovered that the trauma she experienced lasted long after her release from the hospital. She sought PTSD counseling to handle the reoccurring emotions. Cathi suffered survivor's guilt and anniversary depression for many years. Her youthful confidence had eroded into vulnerability when she realized she could not rely on her own strength to run away from danger or perceived danger.

"I had always known that you are more than "your career" – but it was a challenge to not have that "position" anymore. How would I now respond to the question *"and what do you do"?*

"Although I had been raised in the Catholic faith, and attended a catholic girl's school, I did not find myself drawn to a religious path. I had much more connection to the seasons, nature and Universal connectivity. I had never been afraid of death, but rather the process of dying.

I had always had strong close friendships with women, but I was well into my college years before I realized I might actually be a *"lesbian"*. Even then, it was not a major spiritual conflict for me. I just loved. When Kay and I got together, it was just a natural assumption that we were a couple. My mother walked in on us one time, but the topic was never brought up for discussion.

I have always felt the most comfortable with female relationships, and have surrounded myself with women who felt the same. During my healing process, I repeatedly told Kay that she was free to find another relationship, because ours was less than ideal. This situation was definitely more, than what was within the realm of *"normal."* She clearly stated that she could never leave her best friend. We made it through rough patches and have to this day, a strong commitment to our union. Kay went above and beyond in trying to support my journey to *"normal."* She had to do dressing changes, empty bedpans; remove carpeting from our home so I could wheel around, and take me to numerous consults and appointments. She did all this, and still worked full time."

She paused for a time, and then continued. "It was difficult for Kay in another respect. Many, if not most people would ask, "How's Cathi?" They never asked how she was doing. We now call that time the *"Kay Who?"* phenomenon.

So, don't forget, everyone in the house is affected by these traumatic situations."

Cathi was pensive as she continued. "Two situations that are strong in my mind are centered on the time I was still in a wheel chair. We had been active at playing girls softball. Kay wanted me to still feel a part of things, and would put me, the wheel chair and the equipment in our car. She would wheel me out to the field so I could watch the game. On one occasion, the team was short one person. I was still on the roster and upon checking the rules; it didn't say I had to be able to walk. There was a clause that said I needed to be able to stand on my own two feet.

Kay came behind me, grabbed my pants and the back of my shirt...and I stood! The team applauded, and I was rolled out to center field. Kay played right center, and spent the entire game covering both positions, just so we wouldn't have to forfeit the game!

When it was my time to *"bat"*, we designated the coach to run for me. Kay told me to just move the bat a few inches and have it called a strike. I was still dealing with two broken wrists. I had two strikes when a pitch came that was right in the sweet spot. Without thinking, I mustered up enough strength to actually hit it! The coach had to run the bases for me that day, but I was on my way to being *"normal"*.

"In another event we went to the beach. I love the water and longed to get back to snorkeling. Kay rolled my chair to the water's edge and got me into the water. Each wave tossed me around and rolled me up toward the sand. I wanted to feel the waves and water, but it would be a long time before I was back to normal. Kay had to rescue me from the surf."

Cathi shared many other memorable and humorous stories. She still chuckles when she recalls learning to drive an electric wheelchair with a joy stick. She had never used one prior to that time. Then, getting a flat tire on her wheelchair when she was blocks away from where she needed to be. Kay subsequently outfitted her with a tool kit.

Walking the dogs was an adventure every time. If they saw squirrels playing, they would pull her off the paved path and over the bumpy grass. There was the time Cathi got stuck on a 'commode' when her slide board between the wheel chair and the commode slipped onto the floor, just out of her reach. They decided an investment in a portable phone that she could clip to her body was the answer to that scenario. Then there the time she landed in a flower bed when a tire of the wheelchair went off the pavement. Cathi survived all of the challenges, but was left with a sense of deep vulnerability.

"In 15 seconds, life can change who you are and how you relate to the world. Along with those challenges comes a new opportunity for growth and in our case a blended extension of friends from before and after the earthquake.

Our life continues to be an adventure. In the 23 years since the Loma Prieta Earthquake, normal has been re-defined to fit the situations we find ourselves facing. The doctors said *"If I lived, I would never walk again"*. If you met me today you would not comprehend that statement as I am standing and walking on my own, with slight reminders of that earthquake damage to my bones. I have scars both physical (they should have put in zippers) and emotional, but I am more whole today than the expectations of the medical staff that October night."

Cathie met my gaze and continued her story. "I know for a fact, I would not be doing as well as I am today if it wasn't for my partner Kay. There is not enough time to share all she has done, but know she was steadfast in her support. She assisted me with my head injuries by quizzing me with flash cards. I used to manage a million dollar budget, and now I couldn't subtract 9 from 17! She would push me in the wheelchair to events on uneven and hilly terrain. She has unfailingly continued to offer opportunities that would be safe for me to do, yet still be a bit of a stretch.

I often wish that my parents were still alive so that I could share this journey with them. Kay and I are growing old together. It may not be graceful, but we are still together and sharing life. Our relationship has endured over 30 years of challenges and I'm sure there are more in the future but I hope less challenging to experience. We are committed to one another, and our supportive network of women who have encouraged us on our journey to "normal."

Probably not a day goes by that I don't think about how our life was changed by that earthquake, and wonder *"What If."* Could we survive another tragedy? I am clear about my wishes. I don't want life support if there is no hope of recovery. I pray that we never face something like that in our future, but I know that life can change in a moment of time.

I believe we have made an impact on the world because we have found that love is the strongest bond, and it flourishes in feminine energy. I want to change the prejudice and misconceptions about the LGBT community. We do have longevity and commitment and love, even when bad things happen to good people. We are, after all, just people."

Chapter 12
Marriage Equality

Becky Lake & Darlene Bogle
Married but not equal.

A sun faded poster still sits in the front window of our home. It declares to all who walk or drive past, "I believe in Marriage Equality."

It has been almost five years since Prop 8, the same sex marriage initiative for Equality, was passed by voters in California by a narrow margin. Regulations against same sex marriage had been declared unconstitutional, and for four months, over 18,000 gay and lesbian couples had been legally wed in California. We were one of those couples.

We are married in California, in the eyes of God, our families and friends, but still denied the 1,047 rights and protections that go automatically with heterosexual civil marriage. The Federal government doesn't recognize our marriage however, at tax time, we must file individual state returns; joint Federal returns that split our *"community"* assets, taxes and income. This is not equality.

Someday I pray that all persons, straight, gay, bisexual, and transgendered will have equality and be recognized by the federal government. I pray that in California, Prop.8

will be declared unconstitutional and my brothers and sisters will once again be allowed to marry. It really does make a difference.

Why should it matter? Becky and I have been together almost seven years. We've been legally married four of those years. We had a *"commitment"* ceremony in Hawaii seven years ago, but we were not legally married. Our love was strong and we didn't need a piece of paper to say we would be together for the rest of our lives. But, still we were not legally married. If we were traveling to other states, and one of us was hospitalized, we could not legally be allowed access to stay at the others bedside. We took care of the Power of Attorney forms, the Durable power of attorney for health care, adding both names to all real property, and having a will to declare our wishes for the other's future security. But, still we were not legally married.

Now we are married, but only the state acknowledges our union. Why should it matter?

I remember when we were planning our wedding. Becky was in tears when she told me: *"I knew I was gay most of my life. I never thought I would ever have a real wedding."* **It matters.** It feels different to sign a legal document and know that you are partners for life.

Becky's nephew Andy walked us down the aisle. One of Becky's sisters helped with decorations, and supported our public commitment at our church. There were many who did not and still do not acknowledge our relationship, as blessed by God. So, how did we arrive at this marriage experience, and support equality for all people?

BECKY:

She was almost 30 years old when she came to the acceptance that she was a lesbian. She grew up in a strongly religious home, and was hesitant to come out to her parents and sisters. There were years that she felt so isolated and alone because she was different. She had a couple of relationships, but always had to hide their true nature because it was viewed as a *"sin"* in her world.

In 2005 Becky and Darlene fell in love. Becky had been single for 17 years, because she was determined to not settle for someone who did not honor her understanding of God. Relationships born in bar rooms are usually short lived. The next three years were filled with hope that one day we would be able to legally marry.

The courts made some great headway in declaring the ban on same sex marriage as unconstitutional. We were optimistic that our civil rights would be allowed and we could be more than domestic partners. The election of 2008 had a proposition to take it all away, but we felt sure the people of California would stand by **equality.** We picked up our marriage license and planned our wedding for the end of September. That short window of opportunity was a time that we, along with many of our friends, finally got married.

I remember on our wedding day, Becky felt such a glow of acceptance for the first time in her life. We wanted to be a little less traditional for our church wedding with family and friends. We decided to serve not a traditional wedding cake, but lemon meringue pie that was displayed like a cake. It spoke of our uniqueness. And that when life gives you lemons, you can make a pie!

That glow of acceptance all changed when Prop 8 was passed. Becky thought she would be willing to die for this cause just to have that '*acceptance*' again. She contributed financial support, and got involved in political actions to have Prop 8 declared unconstitutional. It soon was revealed that the money to pass Prop 8 was largely through the efforts of the Mormon Church and their headquarters in Utah. Money and Religion were applied to deny us the right to marry.

A long series of court challenges and appeals have done nothing but confirm that same sex marriage should allowed and that it discriminates against an entire class of people. Each time, it is challenged again the court says we should be allowed to marry. Now it is once again scheduled to go to the Supreme Court.

The decision of who should be allowed to marry, made by puffed up people who think they speak for God, has dragged every hope of equality through the mud. It has brought back the feelings of not being accepted and "*less than.*" Becky's hope for justice and equality has grown dimmer yet the glimmer remains, with the passing years and although the passage of Prop 8 broke her heart, her faith and her love for Darlene have grown stronger every day.

DARLENE:

"My heart leaps with joy every time I hear of legislation being passed that will allow gay marriage in other states. I rejoiced when don't Ask-Don't tell was repealed in the military, and when the Defense of Marriage Act was ruled unconstitutional. These are significant, yet small steps toward National Equality. Yet, California has not reinstated the right to marry for same sex couples. Why should it matter?

Becky and I enjoy a legally married status, however many of our friends are prevented from experiencing the same joy we felt on our wedding day. As a minister, I can, and do marry heterosexual couples, but cannot do the same for homosexual couples. It's not just marriage equality that I support, but full equality for all citizens.

My heart longs for the time when gays and lesbians are free to celebrate their love, and to fully understand that God loves them in a radically inclusive way. He longs to celebrate with them, not as shameful outcasts, but as sons and daughters. Why should it matter?

Equality will one day be a reality, but for now, hundreds of my brothers and sisters are treated as second rate baggage. They experience rejection and condemnation on a daily basis. We shouldn't have to battle for our place at God's table, and equality with heterosexual Christian brothers and sisters.

Equality is still a distant dream, but it is a dream that will not die.

Why should it matter? Because justice is the right thing to have happen, and mercy and compassion are qualities of a loving God.

We are all children of the same Creator. Love is not just what I share with Becky, it's how I choose to live out the life of Jesus in this world. Equality is a right, and it's our inheritance.

That's why I fight for equality and civil rights for all."

Chapter 13
GAY CIVIL RIGHTS

Wiggsy Silvetsen LCSW
Gay Civil Rights Activist
San Jose

It has been almost 45 years that Wiggsy Silvetsen has been working for San Jose State University as a faculty counselor; however her influence extends far beyond the SJSU's gay community. She has been called a woman with a strong personality, which she has used to become a voice for the LGBT community in the south bay, and beyond.

Wiggsy says she knew she was a lesbian early in life, but was still in the closet until the early 60's. Those were the days prior to any legal job protections and she knew she could be fired. At one point prior to working for SJSU, she was in fact let go, and she took boycott actions against her employer. It would not be the last time she took a stand against injustice (quoted from the Spartan Daily article of March 19, 2009).

In 1968 she made the decision to be an "out" lesbian, and went to the president of the university, Robert Clark, to make sure there would be no problems with her orientation. He reportedly told her, "I don't care. Just do your job."

She was the only openly lesbian person on campus at the time and it was quite lonely. She filled her hours with active involvement with the black student movement and the women's movement on campus. She moderated encounter groups for African American students in those years, and is proud to have known two historic athletes. There are statutes of Tommie Smith and John Carlos, the gold and bronze medalists in the 200m, 1968 Mexico Olympics. They staged a silent protest against racial discrimination of black people in the United States by receiving their medals with heads bowed and fist raised. Smith, the holder of seven world records raised his right fist to represent black power in America, and Carlos raised his left fist to represent black unity. Together, they formed an arch of unity and power. Within hours, their actions were condemned by the International Olympic Committee.

Thirty years after their protest, the two men were honored for their part in furthering the civil rights movement in America, and today their statues are a perpetual reminder upon San Jose University Campus.

Wiggsy helped to create the first gay support group of SJSU campus. She says, "We had the first gay and lesbian student group in the California State University system. With the work of Paul Wysocki, we managed to deeply disturb the Chancellor who didn't believe that they should allow, "those people" to have their own group on campus." However, it was obvious that the students did not agree with the chancellor, and came together to support the development of a student group and was fully supported by the Associated Students leadership

Another political effort, of which she is quite proud, is the expulsion of the Army and Air Force ROTC, which took about 15 or 16 years of pushing the Academic Senate to abide with the nondiscrimination policy of the CSU. Unfortunately, Congressman Soloman decided that any university that would not allow the ROTC programs on campus would lose all federal funding. This legislation was placed in the federal defense budget, so it sailed through congress. Because of the financial effect this would have on the students, SJSU decided they could not continue the ban. The air force came back to continue their recruiting. Now, of course, with President Obama's change in the law it is no longer a challenge for the lesbian and gay men who are openly "out". Don't ask-Don't tell has been eliminated as a qualification for service.

She is passionate about the rights of people everywhere, especially those who have been marginalized. (Spartan Daily news SJSU March 2009)

One of the equality rights she personally fought for in the California State University system was obtaining health benefits for gay and lesbian workers and spouses that would equal the heterosexual benefits. She states that she spent many years pushing CSU to provide those benefits to the Lesbian and Gay employees. Ultimately, this did happen because of legislation in Sacramento, which required them to implement a program for domestic partner benefits.

Her causes have included the battle for 15 gender neutral bathrooms on campus. She said, "When the budget people went a little crazy, I pointed out that it would involve just changing a sign! It was the cheapest retrofit possible."

Wiggsy feels that we should take time to get to connect with each other and to respect differences without hurting each other. She feels our conversations should extend to groups who do not support gay rights.

She recalls a time when she spent time with Peter Wilkes, the pastor of South Hills Community Church in San Jose. The board of supervisors was deliberating domestic partner rights and Wilkes's congregation was calling the gay community terrible names. Wilkes spoke out and scolded the Christian community, while at the same time affirming his belief that homosexuals were sinners. Wiggsy stated that she disagreed with him on that topic, but appreciated him for being a really nice guy. They attended the board meeting agreeing to disagree, but willing to have a constructive public discourse. She also said she thinks the gay community should reach out to people who are anti-gay. Her interactions continue into the political arena.

Wiggsy was a cofounder of an LGBT political action committee called BAYMEC in 1984. It is a four county political action group co-founded with Ken Yeager in 1984. They have fought for persons with AIDS, and are currently working for Marriage Equality. Wiggsy recently was quoted as saying "Same sex marriage is the essential civil rights issue we are facing today. Gay couples deserve to have the same rights allowed by marriage as heterosexual couples." She was part of the group of gay and lesbian activists appealing to San Jose Mayor Chuck Reed to sign a resolution to support same sex marriage. San Jose is the only big city besides Dallas, whose mayor hasn't signed the statement. (San Jose Mercury News June 4, 2012)

Whether the issues are women and domestic violence, suicide on college campus, health benefits for everyone including the transgendered community or blood drives that discriminate against gay men, you will hear Wiggsy in the crowd calling for justice and equality. Like the civil rights battles of the 1960's, Wiggsy is in this for the long haul. (San Jose Mercury news January 11, 2010)

In September of 2004, the House of Representatives recognized Wiggsy Silvetsen for her achievements as an advocate for over 20 years.

She was one of the founders not only of BAYMEC but Advocates for Lesbian, Gay and Bisexual Youth, and OMNI- Open Mind Network, Inc. which is dedicated to educating organizations about lesbian, gay and bisexual people. She has been named to the "Millennium 100, Pillars of their Communities" by the San Jose Mercury News and received a California State Special Recognition Award for service to the Lesbian and Gay Community

San Jose State University has established a Wiggsy Silvetsen Scholarship to acknowledge those students who have advanced the SJSU LGBT community through their involvement, service, advocacy and/or scholarship on campus.

In June of 2007, Assembly District 21 in California honored her as woman of the year for her fight for our civil rights. I, for one, am glad to know her as an advocate and activist

Chapter 14
SECOND PARENT ADOPTION

Deborah Pugh and Carol Gossett
Near Half Moon Bay, California

Today, there are agencies and attorneys that special-
ize in assisting lesbians with adoptions as single parents,
and as couples, and children have been placed into these
loving homes. Twenty years ago, this was not the case in
California. There were no laws to provide for the protection of both parents when one was the biological parent.
Deborah and Carol were the first same sex couple in San
Mateo County to apply for this "second-parent" adoption.

Their case was a precedent-setting court case, cost-
ing thousands of dollars, to gain the acknowledgment that
Carol was legally the parent of their daughter. Deborah was
the biological mother, and their daughter was conceived
through a known donor, a gay friend of the couple.

Deb and Carol had been in a committed relationship
for 5 years, prior to the birth of their daughter Morgan.
They had planned the pregnancy for two years, doing extensive research and education about home birth. Carol
was with the midwives at the birth, and she cut the cord,

and was the first to hold her daughter. There should have been no question as to parenthood.

However, in 1991 it became apparent that legal documents should be drawn up just in case something happened to Deborah. The doctors had discovered a large ovarian cyst which was life threatening. The doctors delayed surgery for three weeks in order for Deb and Carol to get their wills done, and make arrangements in case of a medical crisis. They consulted with an attorney, where they learned that the wills might not stand up in court in the case of a custody battle. Without a legal adoption, if something happened to Deborah, Carol would have no legal right to raise her own child.

The surgery resulted in a complete hysterectomy. Any hope of having other children was no longer an option. It was clear to Deb and Carol that they needed to move forward with the adoption plans. This type of adoption had never been done in San Mateo County, and the process took a year to finalize. They were assisted by two private attorneys and aided by the NCLR and other gay rights organizations. Their area in Northern California is fairly conservative and this was a new concept in adoptions.

While all the legal concerns were being addressed, the state of California proceeded with the usual adoption process. This included the standard interviews, the home-visits and background checks. The only complaint the social worker noted was that their home was "too child centered."

There was toddler art on all four walls of Morgan's play-room!

It was also during this time that Deb and Carol had to ask the biological father to sign over his legal rights to Morgan. It was a very stressful time for them, as well as for the dad. He indicated that it was hard to sign over his rights to his child, even though he had never expected to be a father. Ultimately, he agreed to sign the release papers.

With the adoption complete and the release signed, the two women were greatly relieved. No matter what might happen to either of them, there was no question about who would raise their daughter. Morgan was aware from an early age that her family was special. She used to tell anyone who would listen, "My mommies are married in their heart." In July 2008, that marriage became a legal reality during the few months before Proposition 8 took away the right to marry. Deb and Carol were one of the 18,000 same sex couples who wed legally in California.

When Morgan was 6 years old she asked if she had a dad. Carol and Deb told her "Yes." She asked if she could meet him. They called him at his home in Louisiana and he agreed to meet her. He flew to California shortly after-wards, to meet Morgan for the first time. She has contin-ued to have contact with him and has maintained a good relationship through the years.

There has never been any conflict with knowing that Carol and Deborah are her parents. Their family of choice (many other gay and lesbian families) has been their support through the years. Many of those people are still dear friends to this day. Carol had no family support at the time neither of Morgan's birth nor during the adoption process. Deborah's family lived across the country in Northern Florida, and initially offered only a cautious verbal support. She had been raised Southern Baptist, and her journey of coming to terms with her sexuality found her at odds with her faith roots. In an effort to bring a sense of community for her daughter, Deborah did embrace the Unitarian Universalist church. After the birth of Morgan, the grandparents fell in love with her. The hesitation was gone, and they shared in all the events of Morgan's life.

The last few years of her mother's life, Deborah's mom suffered from Alzheimer's. She was able to come live with Deborah and Carol for months at a time. Her care was shared with a sister on the east coast. Throughout the progression of the disease, Carol cared for her as if she was her own mother. At the funeral, Carol was a brave pall-bearer for her mother in law. The pastor of the Southern Baptist church was not sure how to react, however she was allowed to participate in the service and it meant a lot to both Deborah and Morgan.

Deborah and Carol have a fierce love for their daughter and both affirm there is no greater love!

So, what was life like for two moms and a daughter? They bought a small ranch in the country where Morgan was raised to be strong and independent. She continues to live her life that way today. She enjoyed horseback riding and competed in rodeos, training and competing for years in English Show Jumping on the west coast and in Canada. She dated and developed healthy relationships. In high school, she was the school valedictorian and also the prom queen. She was just like all her school mates, and considered her life normal here in the Bay Area.

As Deborah reviewed her family history, she recalled that there were other women, unmarried and living with another woman who always were referred to as "that woman she lives with," and their relationships seemed accepted on a certain level.

Deborah has worked at Stanford for many years, while Carol has pursued and enjoyed a life in professional golf. She is currently a golf instructor!

Carol knew from a young age that she was "different" but didn't connect it to being gay. She grew up believing that her life would never include such things as children or PTA. She never had the desire to physically give birth, but when Morgan was born, she loved her as if she had given birth herself. She says, "Having Morgan in my life has been the most enriching and amazing thing I could ever have imagined." That's what parenthood is supposed to be.

They continue to live in a small town community and have discovered that parenting is universal. Everyone goes through ups and downs, they work out conflicts and in the end, they love their children and the children love them. Deb and Carol don't feel it has been unusual to be two mommies "who are married in their hearts."

I can't help but agree.

Chapter 15
LGBT Seniors

Marti Anthony (69 years young)
Trainer/Advocate for Senior LGBT community

The Lesbian, Gay, Bisexual and Transgendered community has become more visible in recent years, and one thing is evident: We are aging. There are unique circumstances that accompany our community as many are now living in retirement homes or nursing facilities.

Marti Anthony is one of over 30 trainers in 16 states that leads classes for care givers and administrators for service providers. She has been on the advisory council serving older adults, as well as facilitating cultural sensitivity classes for those who serve the LGBTQ community.

Her work is part of the aging Division of Boulder County, "Project Visibility" used throughout the United States and Canada.

Her training classes address homophobia by the staff, as well as how to meet the needs of those with Alzheimer's disease. There has been an increasing awareness that many heterosexual caregivers experience homophobia and religious prejudice due to a lack of basic information. They have a "fear of catching it," although homosexuality is neither a choice nor something you can catch. Proper information and education goes a long way in helping organizations treat their clients with respect and dignity in their senior years.

From her home base in Port Townsend Washington, Marti has become a voice throughout all of Western Washington. She worked on the mental Health board in Port Townsend for a number of years. All of the same needs found in the heterosexual society are present in the homosexual community. As we move forward into our senior years, addressing these issues with compassion and knowledge is crucial.

Marti has put her degree in gerontology to good use. She worked for over four years with seniors to provide Paratransit to doctor's appointments. Her degree in Sociology has also served her well. She has learned to work with senior LGBTQ clients to equip them to have their papers in order for Wills, and end of life issues. Many clients find that their support system has decreased through the years, and there is no one to provide that guidance.

One such organization that is supported by the Federal Government is SAGEUSA It is the country's oldest and largest organization serving LGBT Elders It was founded in 1978 in New York and works with the National Resource Center on LGBT Aging. It is a non-profit supported by Federal grants and public donations. In order to end the invisibility of aging and older adults in the LGBT community, SAGE supports local LGBT leadership and older adult advocates as powerful engines for positive change within communities. SAGENET affiliates strengthen local work, increase visibility, and provide a national network of programs and services for LGBT older adults around the country. It is a clearing house of information.

One area of increasing concern is the Transgender community.

Many older adults face profound challenges and experience striking disparities in areas such as health and health care access, physical and mental health, employment, housing and more. Research and experience also reveal that many transgender elders routinely encounter both a health care system and a national aging network that are ill-prepared to provide culturally competent care and services and create residential environments that affirm the gender identities and expressions of transgender older people. With a growing older transgender population, there is an urgent need to understand the challenges that can threaten financial security, health and overall well-being. It is often difficult depending upon the process of the change, and whether they have had sexual reassignment surgery. If they enter a facility as "Robert" but do not have the genitals of a "Robert", they are often discriminated against or ridiculed. Sub quality care is often the norm for minorities, and often the partners are denied access to their sick or ailing partner.

Education alone cannot remedy the situation, but it is a starting place. Awareness can facilitate compassion and make the environment safe and welcoming to LGBT older adults. Things like being comfortable with language and common terms related to the LGBT community will challenge the common assumptions and stereotypes of the straight community. As the need grows to serve seniors, so do the service organizations partnering with the National Resource Center on LGBT Aging. It was established in 2010 through a Federal grant from the U.S. Department of Health and Human Services. Currently, such groups as the American Society on Aging, FORGE Transgender Aging Network, the LGBT Aging project, National Aging Pacific Center on Aging, National Association of Area Agencies on Aging, National Caucus & Center on Black Aged, Inc., National Hispanic Council on Aging and Southeast Asia Resource Action Center are all partnered to provide services.

So, how did Marti find herself drawn into this type of occupation in her senior years? We should start in her childhood.

When she was 11 years old, she knew she was gay. Her mother was deeply religious and felt the need to "cure" her of these homosexual tendencies. Marti was sent to Vashti, an all-girls school in Georgia. This only reinforced her commitment to keep her feelings hidden and act as if she was like the other girls. Inside her heart, she knew she would never be "like them."

She was 23 when she met and married her husband. She identified as bisexual in her mind, realizing that she was not free to express her homosexuality. They had five children, and her life was filled with raising the children and being a "wife". Today, she is divorced from her husband, and all of her children are aware of her sexual orientation and have accepted her for the woman she is, a lesbian.

Her duel life lasted for 30 years and on several occasions, she sought deliverance from homosexuality. It never worked for her, and finally she accepted her natural, sexual orientation and entered into a committed lesbian relationship.

The dream of being loved and accepted as a lesbian was soon shattered. Her partner was abusive, verbally and physically. She stayed in that relationship for 5 years, believing she deserved the treatment because she was "queer". She was subjected to not only the domestic violence but sexual assault.

Through counseling and therapy, she was able to leave that relationship, and found a loving and caring companion, Evelyn, who accepted her and encouraged her to find her own voice as a lesbian and a senior within the LGBT community. They have been together for 12 years.

In finding her own voice, Marti is now able to help others. In all the complexity of navigating the social and medical challenges that face gay and lesbian people, Marti is committed to serve her sisters and brothers on their journey.

Chapter 16
Mini Snapshots:

It has been a delight to share stories of women who have been part of some aspect of history. As lesbians, I am impressed that we have been and continue to be a significant part of the fabric of society. Our lives are present at events, because we are part of the world, not because we are lesbians, but simply because we exist!

YVETTE FLUNDER
It occurred to me that I have been very blessed to know some outstanding women who continue to make History by how they live. One such woman is Bishop Yvette Flunder. She is an African American woman who is senior pastor of a UCC church in San Francisco. The City of Refuge is host to programs that feed the homeless; clothe the less fortunate; have the only all Transgender choir in the country, and reach out nationally and internationally to those with aids.

From the outside, city of Refuge in San Francisco doesn't resemble a typical church. Truth be told, it is anything but typical. From the moment you walk through the door, you are made welcome and it is apparent that diversity is not only embraced, but celebrated.

Bishop Yvette A. Flunder and Shirley Miller have been a couple since May 19, 1984. Together they lead City of Refuge at 1025 Howard Street San Francisco, CA 94103. Bishop

Flunder describes a typical service as "Bapta-Metho-cos-tal", incorporating faith traditions from Baptist, Methodist and Pentecostal.

City of Refuge United Church of Christ is an inten-tionally radically inclusive ministry welcoming all persons regardless of race, color, ancestry, age, gender, affectional orientation, and those who are differently-abled. Worship includes prayer, preaching and songs from many faith tradi-tions. They have been connected with the United Church of Christ since 1991.

Everyone who enters those doors is included in the ministry. If you sing, you join the choir, if you serve; you can participate in one of the 30 outreach positions that service the community. Yvette says, "it is our ministry to improve the quality of life in a real and tangible way.' She believes the reason the ministries are a success is because the indi-viduals who have come from the same place as those they serve, and are helping run them. No matter where you were or what you were involved with before you came to City of Refuge, there is a place for you.

I remember Bishop Yvette preaching at a conference a year or so ago. She ended her talk with, "God has a big table...and all His children are welcome there!"

The city of Refuge is making history, and making a difference for the LGBT community and all who have been marginalized by society.

DR. SUZANNE DIBBLE

Suzanne Dibble, RN, DNSc. makes a difference! She has been one of the foremost researchers in Lesbian Health. Her interest in research came from her clinical practice and experiences as a nurse. For more than four decades, she has provided care and explored care practices for individuals with chronic illnesses, especially cancer. Her primary commitment has been to research and to developing evidence on which to base clinical practice.

In addition, Sue has undertaken to help nurses and other health care providers deliver care in a culturally appropriate manner by editing two books: Lesbian Health 101- Dibble, SL & Robertson, PA (2010); and Culture and Clinical Care-Lipson, JA & Dibble, SL (2005). She has also coauthored a book directed at clinicians: "Lesbian, gay, bisexual and transgender cultures: What the clinician needs to know". (2009) Eliason M, Dibble SL, De Joseph JF, and Chinn PL.

Dr. Dibble has written more than 120 articles.

Sue is a co-founder of the Lesbian Health and Research Center at the University of California San Francisco.

The Center was formed in September 1999 after the Institute of Medicine published a report-titled *Lesbian Health Research Priorities.*

Dibble stated. "That information legitimized the decision that this was the time and place for a Center and that it would be appropriate." Two of the most significant conclusions of the report were that additional data is required to determine if lesbians are at higher risk for certain health problems; and there are significant barriers to conducting research on lesbian health, including lack of funding. That lack of financial support has limited the development of more sophisticated studies. Research about lesbian health will help advance scientific knowledge and will also benefit other population groups.

Dr. Dibble is part of the Gay and Lesbian Medical Association, the American Society on Aging, and the International Council on Women's Health.

She has been given many awards, too numerous to list but just two of the awards are a "2003 Visionary Award for Achievement in Lesbian Health", given by Lyon-Martin Women's Health Services and a "Lifetime Achievement Award", given by the Gay and Lesbian Medical Association. She has also been recognized as a Senior Leader for the State of California.

Her efforts to increase awareness of LGBTQ issues and facilitate clinical care, especially for lesbians are a hallmark of her career. Her contributions continue in her retirement with the co-founding of Oakmont Rainbow Women in 2011 in Santa Rosa, Ca.

REV. DEBORAH JOHNSON

Rev. Deborah Johnson is making a difference! She is an African American and the founding minister and president of Inner Light Ministries in Soquel California. It is an Omni-faith outreach ministry dedicated to teaching the practical application of universal spiritual principles in all of life's circumstances.

The church where they meet was formerly an Assembly of God church until about 20 years ago. It was the church I attended when I went to Bible College. I shared with Rev. Johnson about a prophetic word that was spoken back in the 1980's about that church being a "lighthouse, shining a beacon of light to the community, then to the state, then to the world." That word was given when it seemed that the Assemblies of God would be that beacon. However, Rev. Johnson brought out a lighthouse that she had been given when she first moved into the church. Like so many prophetic words, the truth has its own timetable. The message of Inner Light Ministries shines around the globe as a vision. Spirit is proclaimed as our Creator.

She holds a vision of oneness, beyond creed and doctrine and feels particularly called to heal the sense of separation between those adhering to conservative and progressive ideologies.

A life-long social justice activist, Rev. Deborah was a successful participant in two landmark cases in California – one set precedent for the inclusion of sexual orientation in the state's Civil Rights Bill, the other defeated the challenge to legalizing domestic partnerships. A voice for compassion, equality, and reconciliation, her primary focus has been on coalition building, conflict resolution, public policy development, and cultural sensitivity awareness.

Rev. Deborah Johnson along with Director of music, Valerie Joi Fiddmont, was honored to be part of the national choral performing music at Carnegie Hall in 2011. The Inner Light Choir was part of the 270-voice choir for this program. That is just one of the ways that this beacon of light is reaching the world.

She has been honored for her past and present work in the LGBT community, and is in high demand as a speaker, nationally and internationally.

Deborah was interviewed in a Documentary film, "God and Gays, Bridging the Gap", which explores the religious struggle reconciling sexuality and spirituality. It gets into the heads and hearts of people who inhabit the world of homosexuality and religious traditions.

She appeared as well in: "Jumpin' the Broom" which shares the stories of four black gay and lesbian couples – two male and two female – and analyzes their views on love, commitment, relationships, marriage and religion. Jumpin' the Broom delivers engaging characters, poignant images and, above all, conveys hope.

"Growing up gay, nobody ever thought that it was possible to find someone that you could live your life with. My heart would break when I realized that because of being gay, I was denied so many of the rights that heterosexual couples enjoy. I have lived my life to take a stand against discrimination and pray that the next generation will have more freedom than this generation."

Deborah Johnson is making history as well as being part of the LGBT history for Equality.

Judy Dlugacz
Olivia-Music and Travel

Back in 1973 Judy had a vision to create a women's record label, Olivia Records.

We were introduced to such lesbian artists as Meg Christian and Ginny Berson. The lesbian community was largely invisible and Judy wanted to create a forum where women could find their voice. And find their voice they did, by the hundreds who flocked to concerts around the country, including Carnegie Hall! She wanted to change the world through lesbian-feminism, and many artists joined her vision.

In 1990 her vision expanded to merge music, comedy and travel, and she offered the first all-women's cruise. She chartered a ship, sent out a mass mailing to the women on Olivia Records mailing list, and signed up 600 women. The ship booked quickly, so she decided to have back to back trips, and 1200 lesbians began to enjoy the experience of travel in the company of women only.

Olivia is one of the largest charters for Holland America lines, and the impact upon the travel industry has changed in how they view gay travelers. Olivia has also become an advocate for how companies deal with their gay employees.

The trips have been taken around the world, and have not always been met with an extravagant welcome! I remember in the early years of Olivia Cruises, the Bahamas were a popular destination. In Nassau, the ship was met by a small demonstration that was intent upon expressing their displeasure with homosexuality. The funny thing was the demonstrators stood on the pier singing Christian songs. They were shocked, when the women on the ship also knew the hymns and began to sing back to them. The protest ended when the demonstrators just walked away.

Judy contacted the head of tourism and requested an apology from the Prime Minister of the Bahamas. Not only did she get the apology, but the following week he called a press conference to declare that everyone is welcome, and specifically, all gay people are welcome.

Judy discovered that "gay money" made an impact on tourism, and that has been historic. Women now have a voice and are no longer invisible and are speaking out on all kinds of issues. 2013 will be the 40th year of Olivia's influence and some huge celebrations are planned. To be a part of history, visit Olivia.com or call 1-800-631-6277.

Marsha Stevens-Pino
Singer-Song writer

If you were around in the late 1960's to early 70's...you would have been aware of the Jesus People movement. Many of the hippies in Southern California found God through the outreach of Calvary Chapel in Costa Mesa California. It was a revival that soon spread across the country. The converts were often long haired, barefoot kids who experienced God's love for the first time. They attended Bible studies almost every night, and couldn't get enough of the word of God, which they shared with every person they met.

The music of the day exploded with the birth of Maranatha Music. It was at this time, a musical group was formed, called "Children of the Day". Marsha was part of that group, and her song, "For Those Tears I died" became one of the best known Christian folk songs of the 1970s. That song spoke to hearts everywhere, and was published in numerous hymnals and songbooks around the country. Marsha was often referred to as the "Mother of Contemporary Christian music"

After a seven year marriage to Russ Stevens, and producing six albums with him, they divorced. Marsha, in an effort to be true to herself, came out as a lesbian. She was ostracized and condemned by the Christian music world.

After a period of searching for a new church home, Marsha joined the Metropolitan Community Church, and formed "Born Again Lesbian Music" (BALM Ministries). She began to use her music to proclaim the love of Jesus to lesbian, gay, bisexual and transgender communities. In 1987 she recorded her first album since leaving Children of the Day, entitled "Free to Be". She continues to write and record her music, speaking to the journey of being Christian and gay.

The transition from being a celebrity in the Christian music industry to being an "out" lesbian has not been easy. She has received cruel and hateful letters along with pages of "For Those Tears I died" shredded and stuffed in the envelope.

She has been shunned by the Christian music world; her songs are not played on Christian radio stations, and her albums are not carried by Christian music stores. In spite of this, her music largely focuses on the grace of God and love of Jesus to the LGBT community.

Marsha and her spouse, Cindy Stevens-Pino have begun a music ministry training school for LGBT Christians that is based at their home Church, The King of Peace in St. Petersburg Florida.

Marsha continues to write from her heart and share her music with those who have also been wounded, rejected and shunned by the Christian world. She is making a difference to any who hear and listen to her words.

Marsha can be contacted at www.BalmMinistries.net for speaking engagements; CD's and encouraging words!

SALLY RIDE
Astronaut

On July 23, 2012 the world was saddened to hear of the death of Sally Ride from pancreatic cancer. She was the first woman Astronaut and youngest American to travel in space. It was 1983 when she first made history with that landmark space flight. She continues to make history with an announcement after her death when her obituary was posted. Most of the world was surprised a couple of days later to learn she was a lesbian which she revealed in the obituary she co-wrote with her life partner of 27 years, Tam O'Shaughnessy,

Sally and Tam were private people; however a small circle of friends and family had long been aware of their same-sex relationship and had embraced them and their lives together.

Sally was 61 at the time of her death from pancreatic cancer.

Episcopal Bishop Gene Robinson, who was the first openly gay Bishop in the Anglican world, spoke in support of her choice to not come out publically. "We both grew up in a time when coming out was unthinkable." He went on to say, that "Sally was a tremendous role model for all young girls who had an interest in science and wanted to achieve goals that had been unavailable to them until Sally set the new standard of achievement".

No other astronaut of any nation has ever come out as gay. No active public sports figures in any pro league has come out as gay, however some retired players have done so. Many public figures simply choose to remain private in their personal lives. Sally Ride was one of those private individuals. She inspired and challenged young women to excel in science by forming a company, Sally Ride Science, to promote science education among young people. Her sexual orientation simply was not an issue.

According to a recent study by the Human Rights Campaign, 51% of gay, lesbian, transgender and bisexual workers hide their sexual identity. Fred Sainz, the HRC vice president for communications said his initial reaction to the revelation was, "What a shame that we didn't learn of this while she was alive." Upon pondering the information further, he said, "the fact it was acknowledged in death will still be a powerful message to all Americans about the contributions of their LGBT counterparts."

Sally Ride will always be a significant part of history and her pride in paving the way for young girls to dream big dreams is a great achievement. Her life is much greater than a mini-snapshot; however this chapter would not be complete without her.

EDIE WINDSOR AND THEA SPYER
The Battle against DOMA

Their deeply moving story is told in the documentary, "Thea and Edie: A very long Engagement," distributed by Breaking Glass Pictures.

The love affair began in 1962, and lasted 44 years until the death of Thea from Multiple Sclerosis on February 5 2009. Thea had been diagnosed at age 45 and had lived with the chronic and progressive disease until her 73rd year.

Edie was born in Philadelphia and grew up there. She got married very young then realized it wasn't what she wanted. She moved to New York in 1950.

Thea was born in 1931 in Amsterdam Holland, into a Jewish family. In 1939, her family moved to England during the war and were of a small percentage of Jews who survived the persecution. They were a family of wealth, and in 1940, they were able to move to the United States. Shortly afterwards, she was put into counseling and the therapist told her parents that she would outgrow her tendency toward homosexuality. That never happened! In 1963, she earned her degree in Clinical Psychology. She was able to continue in that occupation during her years of dealing with M.S.

Edie went to NYU and earned a degree in computer science at the beginning of the computer age. She realized she was attracted to women, and began to frequent the bars. She was from the upper middle class of Manhattan and never told her mother of her attraction to women. Her family was very homophobic.

When she met Thea the dance began. Actually, they loved to dance and seemed to just fit together perfectly. Even when Thea's disease confined her to a wheelchair, they would dance. When Thea had water therapy, and had to be lowered into the pool, they would dance. They were deeply in love and dancing was their greatest joy. Edie tells of placing a magnet on their refrigerator that reads: DON'T POSTPONE JOY. They lived by that motto.

In 1967 there was no opportunity for same sex marriage, but Thea wanted to formalize their love. She got down on her knee in the car and asked Edie to marry her. In lieu of a ring which would create too many questions, she presented Edie with a diamond brooch, pinned close to Edie's heart. They knew it's meaning, without having to explain a ring to co-workers or family.

Edie says that in 1969, Stonewall changed her life. It was the first time the gay community took a stand against the oppression of the police and society. The riots that followed gave strength and hope for acceptance. It wouldn't be until 1993 that Domestic Partnerships were recognized in New York. Of course, they registered. However, they still wanted a legal marriage.

As Thea's disease progressed, they realized that Thea might not live to see marriage equality become a reality. On May 22, 2007, they went to Canada and were lawfully married as partners for life. Thea passed away in 2009 and Gay marriage became legal in New York, in 2011.

Almost immediately, Edie was presented with a tax bill of over 350,000 on estate assets that certainly would not apply in a heterosexual marriage! They were legally married and should have been able to shield at least 3.5 million dollars in assets.

DOMA's Section 3 defines marriage as a legal union between one man and one woman. President Barak Obama declared DOMA unconstitutional in 2012, and a federal court in New York ruled that Edie should be refunded the estate tax that she was forced to pay.

At age 83, Edie has been joined by the ACLU to challenge DOMA in the Supreme Court and secure equality and civil rights for everyone. The goal is for federal recognition of same-sex marriage, and that every American will enjoy the same rights of citizenship.

It really is about time, and Edie is sure that Thea would agree. I know that thousands of Americans agree that Equality is past due, and are hoping that justice will prevail at last and all Americans can marry and have that marriage recognized.

KATHY BALDOCK
A straight ally

Kathy Baldock makes a difference in our history and is very involved in the LGBT struggle for equality! She is a straight ally working in the LGBT community, known for her blog, "CanyonWalker @ CanyonwalkerConnections. com."

In her own words: "I am a straight Evangelical Christian walking a path with my God and striving to follow the examples of Jesus. I became a Christian in 1984 within one month of returning to a faith community after a 15 year hiatus. While listening to a sermon at a local Evangelical church, the Gospel just made sense to me. I wanted something far bigger than I, to direct me. I began to see my calling as one to: loosen the chains of injustice, untie the cords of the yoke, set the oppressed free and break every yoke. Isaiah 58 states that then, you will be called "repairer of the breach."

My purpose is to educate and create dialogue between the Christian Church and the LGBT Christian community. My own questioning and doubts on other personal issues caused me to wonder if what I had been told about the gay, lesbian, bisexual and transgender communities was accurate. It was here that I was more receptive to the calling by God to be sensitive to the heart and voices of His LGBT children.

After six years of ministering in this very messy spot in and out of the churches, I am now an advocate to the LGBT community for equality and inclusion in Christian churches. I write, speak, educate, listen and dialogue. OH, there is lots of dialogue! I am open to engaging church leaders and staff in conversation about the treatment and inclusion of all people into the Kingdom and Family of God, with equality.

So, why is my ministry called "Canyon Walker Connections"? I hike a *lot* in some canyons near my home in the Northern Sierra. I've done this daily for a few decades. It is on these canyon dirt and snowy trails that I talk to and listen to God and the Holy Spirit. Trails have become my sacred place.

In the spiritual realm, It also seems I walk, in the not-so-lovely space between two groups: the church and the LGBT Christian communities I bring the message of a non-discriminating, Biblical Jesus, the Grace Giver Supreme into that place of dialogue and tension where many of us feel uncomfortable or have ignored altogether.

No matter where you may be on this path, there is something for you here – encouragement and challenge, education and insights.

Yes, I really am straight, a total zero on the Kinsey Scale of sexual orientation. I have two straight adult children and no close LGBT family members. I love a man who works with the poor and homeless. God really did call me and put me here for such a time as this.

Until God shifts me, I will keep on walking in the divide hoping to repair the breach between the church and the lesbian, gay, bisexual, and transgender Christian community.

Please friend me on Facebook, and go to my blog for resources on how to have this conversation with family and friends. Pray for my journey, and I will pray for yours as we walk together in this world."

Kathy Baldock - Canyonwalker.

Epilogue

Kate Clinton, a lesbian comic, recently ended her one woman stand up show by saying: "We are all part of history."

Once again my memory was flooded with thoughts of the Peoples Park in the 1960's, in Berkeley California. I was there. I thought about Haight/Ashbury in the 1960's. I was there. I remembered the first gay pride parade in San Francisco in 1970. I was there. I remember walking with the MCC church, my first "out" connection of being Christian and gay.

My life experiences have included contact with one of the infamous Charles Manson family members. I was reminded that not all events in history are ones that we remember with fondness. A man named Bruce Davis, who had become a Christian in prison, was looking for someone to correspond with and perhaps come visit. Theology teachers from Bethany Bible College ask me if I would correspond with Bruce. I agreed to do so, and made several in-person visits. He was involved in the Shorty Shea and Gary Hindman murders at the Spahn Ranch in Southern California. We became quite fond of one another during the year we wrote and visited, however he wanted a relationship that would go somewhere, and I knew that I needed to be upfront about my being a Christian lesbian. We finally stopped our visits, and he eventually married another woman who had been writing to him.

Another historic connection was when I was in college, I decided to move to Los Angeles and work for Teen Challenge. Rev. David Wilkerson from New York had made inroads to the gang and drug world there, and Teen Challenge Ministries had sprung up across the country. During the six months I worked in Los Angeles, I met David and Nicky Cruz when they came to work with us on the streets. This era of the 60's was a historic outreach for teen drug and gang evangelism.

In the late 1970's as I struggled with my sexual orientation, I began an affiliation with Exodus International- a reparative therapy ex-gay outreach that has grown to over 120 ministries. The harm that has been done to lesbian and gay people through the years is Historic. I directed a ministry during the 1980s that promoted "pray the gay away", and became a spokesperson for Exodus on a national level. I appeared on national television shows like Oprah, Jerry Springer, the CBS 48 hour show, as well as Sally Jesse Raphael. I was part of that history until 1991.

In 2007 I joined with Beyond Ex-Gay for a historic apology at the Los Angeles gay and lesbian center for the harm that I, and other former exodus leaders had done by telling lies. I apologized for telling individuals and families that they needed to change their sexual orientation in order to be accepted by God. That apology went viral on the internet and has helped to heal many who have viewed it.

I am still realizing that history of some sort occurs in our lives all the time. Whether it was the publication of MS magazine over 40 years ago, that highlighted feminist ideas, or the passing of Title IX which resulted in women gaining the right to participate fully in sports, historic events occur all the time. Title IX influenced the way both men and women view the idea of women and athletics.

The women I have highlighted in this book have made, and continue to make history on both a local and national level. I believe like Kate Clinton stated, "We are all part of history." Our individual history as lesbians may not be well known, but we make a difference to those who know us. Every time we speak out against injustice and for equality, we become part of history. I am thankful for the activists who have come before me, and the opportunity to share some of their stories.

I am thankful for the opportunity to view life events through the lavender keyhole and introduce my readers to my sisterhood of women who make a difference just because we exist!

If you are a lesbian and would like your story considered for my next book, contact me at Turtlehrt@aol.com.

Made in the USA
Charleston, SC
17 November 2012

HARPER **Chapters**

TROUBLE at TABLE 5

#3:
The Firefly Fix

by **Tom Watson**

illustrated by
Marta Kissi

HARPER
An Imprint of HarperCollinsPublishers

Dedicated to Jacob (IASPOWYA)

Library of Congress Control Number: 2020936259
ISBN 978-0-06-295347-6 — ISBN 978-0-06-295346-9 (paperback)

Typography by Torberg Davern
20 21 22 23 24   PC/LSCC   10 9 8 7 6 5 4 3 2 1

First Edition

Table of Contents

CHAPTER ONE
A STRANGE LIGHT

IT WAS BEDTIME on Tuesday.

But I wasn't in bed.

"Mom! Dad!" I called from the top of the stairs.

"Yes, Molly?" Mom called back.

"There's a strange light outside!" I spoke loud enough to reach all the way to the living room. Mom and Dad like to read down there at night.

"What's strange about it?" Dad said loudly.

"It's like a long, straight beam of light," I answered.

"What color is it?" Mom asked.

"Just white," I said. "It's pretty far away. It's not like blue or red or anything."

"What else is strange?" asked Dad.

"It shoots across the sky every six seconds," I yelled.

"Well, it's an even number, anyway," Mom called. "That's good, right?"

"Right," I called back.

My parents know I like even numbers

way more than odd numbers. Because with odd numbers, there's always something left over. And what are you supposed to do with something that's left over? That just doesn't make sense to me.

Dad called, "We're on the way!"

When they got to my room, Mom, Dad, and I watched the light move across the sky from my window.

"What is it?" I asked.

"Looks like a searchlight," Dad said.

"What's a searchlight?"

"It's a real powerful beam of light," Dad started to explain. "You know the spotlight the school uses for the holiday play every year?"

"The one up in the balcony?" I asked.

"Yes," Dad said and nodded. "A searchlight is like that, only a hundred times—maybe a thousand times—more powerful."

SPOTLIGHT

SIMON AS WORLD'S SKINNIEST SANTA

"How come it moves in a circle like that?" I asked. "How come it goes around once every six seconds?"

"It must be on a rotating platform," Mom answered. She pointed her index finger up in the air and turned it slowly.

"Why is it there?"

"I'm not sure," Dad answered and shrugged his shoulders. "It's kind of an old-fashioned thing, to be honest. I haven't seen one in years. Searchlights are used to attract people."

"Like if there was a traveling circus in town," Mom said, helping out. "They would use a searchlight to get people to come to the circus. The idea was that people would be curious about the light in the sky, follow it, and then have fun at the circus."

"Great example," Dad said.

"A circus would be awesome!" I exclaimed. "Do you think that's what it is?"

"I doubt it," Dad answered. "There aren't too many traveling circuses anymore."

"Bummer," I said. "Then what *is* over there?"

"I don't know," Dad said. He pulled down the window shade while Mom fluffed my pillows. "But it's bedtime now."

But I didn't get into bed. No way.

"Do you really think I can go to sleep without knowing *exactly* where that searchlight is?" I asked. "And *why* it's there?"

It was quiet for two seconds while Mom and Dad looked at each other.

Then Dad laughed.

"All right, Molly," he said. "We'll take you there. Get a hoodie to put over your pj's. It's chilly for a June night. And put on some sneakers."

"Yay!" I yelled and jumped up and down four times. "Thanks, Dad!"

YOU'VE ALREADY READ 534 WORDS. OFF TO A GREAT START!

1

CHAPTER TWO

IT'S ANNOYING!

WE DIDN'T TALK much as we drove. Dad concentrated on getting us to that searchlight. Mom helped by watching the light and telling him when to turn. I was busy looking out the window. Sometimes when I look out the car window, I'm so busy that I forget to blink. And I have to say in my brain, *"Blink, Molly, blink."*

We got to the searchlight.

It wasn't a cool traveling circus.

It was a boring car dealership.

Dad parked, turned to me, and asked, "How many signs did we pass?"

"Thanks for asking," I said and smiled at him. "We passed thirty-three signs."

"Thirty-three?" Mom asked. "That's an odd number. Do you want to drive around for a minute so you can finish on an even number?"

"No," I said and shook my head. "I want to see the light now."

The searchlight was strapped to the back of a big truck. There was a large red metal box on the ground next to the truck. A bunch of thick rubber cables ran from the red box to the searchlight. We walked closer. The metal box hummed and vibrated.

"What's the big red box for?" I asked.

"I think it's a generator," Dad said. "It runs on gasoline. That searchlight needs a lot of power. If it was just plugged into an outlet, it would probably knock out the electricity in the whole town."

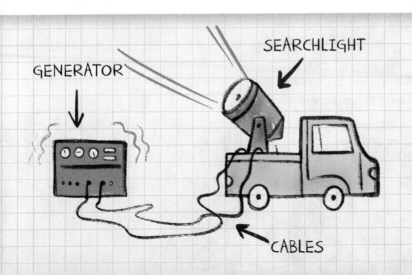

GENERATOR

SEARCHLIGHT

CABLES

"Like during that big storm last year?"

"Exactly," Mom answered.

We stopped about ten feet from the searchlight. The circular motion was calming and rhythmic. I could feel my head rotate on my neck slightly as I watched it turn and turn.

"Why is it here?" I asked. "At a car dealership?"

Dad said quietly, "You're about to find out."

Because I was mesmerized

12

by that rotating light, I hadn't noticed that a woman had walked up to us.

"I'm Hannah," the woman said. She had a name tag on her shirt. "We've got a big sale going on this week. Great cars. Zero percent financing. Are you interested in upgrading to a new model?"

"No, I'm not," Dad answered politely.

Mom said, "Our daughter saw the searchlight and was curious about it."

Hannah leaned down to look at me. "And what is your name?" she asked.

"Molly Dyson."

"Well, Molly Dyson," Hannah said and smiled, "what do you think of our big light in the sky?"

"I think it's annoying," I said. "I'm awake because I had to find out what it was. And it's Tuesday. It's a school night. My friends Rosie, Simon, and I have to come up with a project tomorrow for the science fair—and make it work by Friday

night. So I should really be sleeping." Hannah seemed a little surprised at my answer. She said, "I'm sorry about that, Molly."

"May I ask you a question?" I said.

"Of course."

"Did you know that you can spell your name backward and forward?"

"I *did* know that," Hannah answered.

"Can I ask you another question?"

"Sure."

"When are you going to turn the light off?"

"We're open late this week because of the sale, Molly. We close at ten o'clock," Hannah said. "We'll turn it off a little before then."

"Okay," I said and took Mom's hand. We turned around to go to the car. "Bye."

Dad laughed. Every now and then he laughs a little bit at me. He just thinks I'm funny sometimes.

CHAPTER THREE

STUCK IN MY HEAD

I **STOOD AT** my window and watched the searchlight make its circular pattern across the sky, flashing by my window every six seconds.

Just like Hannah promised, the searchlight went off right before ten o'clock.

I hadn't realized how much brighter the night was with the searchlight. Now that it was off, I could see how dark it was.

There was no moonlight or starlight—it was cloudy out.

Oh, and there were fireflies. In our backyard. A bunch of them.

How could something so little blink so brightly?

The searchlight needed a big red gasoline-powered generator to shine its light.

Fireflies don't have generators.

The searchlight is used to attract people.

Fireflies use their light to attract other fireflies. I thought. I didn't know that for

 sure.

There was something there. Right at the edge of my mind. Something needed to be figured out. Something needed to be done.

I climbed into bed.

But I didn't fall asleep for quite a while.

Something was stuck in my head.

Fireflies.

CHAPTER FOUR

THE FIREFLY PROBLEM

I HOPED THAT the fireflies would get unstuck by school the next day. I knew I should really be thinking about the science fair.

But the fireflies didn't get unstuck.

"There's something I have to talk to you guys about," I told Rosie and Simon on the way to lunch. "It's important."

We hustled through the cafeteria line, got our food fast, and sat at a table by ourselves. For lunch that day we had chicken nuggets, a banana, and a scoop of mashed potatoes.

I like bananas because they're the same color on the outside and the inside. The outside is dark yellow and the inside is light yellow. No problem.

I don't like fruits that are one color on the outside but a totally different color on the inside. Like watermelon is green on the outside, but red on the inside. Or apples are red on the outside, but white on the inside.

It just doesn't seem very honest.

You know what I mean?

So I like bananas. I broke mine into eight bite-size pieces.

"Rosie," I said. "Can I ask you something?"

"Here it comes," Simon said.

"What?" I asked. "Here *what* comes?"

"Simon and I could tell something was bugging you," Rosie said. "We just figured it was the science fair. I know you're worried about coming up with a project. We are too."

I smiled. They knew me so well.

Simon asked, "So what is it?"

"It's not the science fair," I answered. "It's fireflies. I want Rosie to tell me everything she knows about them."

"First of all, fireflies aren't flies at all," Rosie began. I knew she'd have good information. She's *so* good at science. That was one reason why we weren't, like, totally panicked about the fair on Friday. We had Rosie on our team.

"They're beetles. When they flash their light, that's called bioluminescence."

I asked, "What else?"

"It's okay to catch fireflies, but you shouldn't keep them for more than a day. And you don't need to poke holes in the jar. Lots of people do that, but you don't have to. You just need to drop something wet in the jar. They like moist air. Their light can be yellow, green, or orange."

I took a banana bite and asked, "Why do they flash their light?"

"To attract a mate," Rosie answered.

"That's what I thought."

"Awesome," Simon said. "I've always wanted to learn about the romantic habits of fireflies."

"Really?" I asked.

"No."

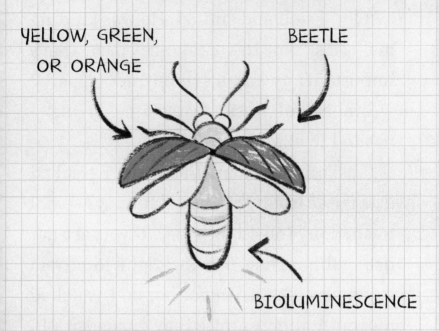

YELLOW, GREEN, OR ORANGE

BEETLE

BIOLUMINESCENCE

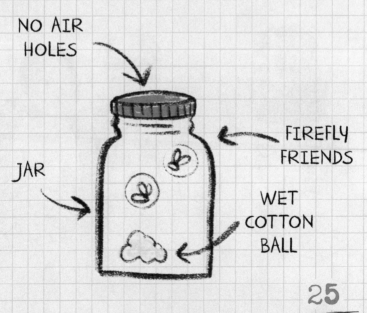

NO AIR HOLES

FIREFLY FRIENDS

JAR

WET COTTON BALL

"Oh," I said and smiled. He was kidding me. "It's not the romance part that's important anyway. It's the attraction part."

Simon and Rosie just stared at me. I needed to explain.

"Last night, Mom, Dad, and I tracked down a searchlight in Bucktown," I said. I pushed my tray to the side. "It was at a car dealership. They use the light to attract customers. After we got home, I watched out my window until they turned it off.

When the searchlight went out, it got really dark. I saw a bunch of fireflies and I started wondering about something. And it got stuck in my head."

"Here it comes," Simon said.

Rosie nodded.

"Searchlights are big and bright and made to attract lots of people," I said and stopped. I leaned toward my best friends. "I want to make firefly light bigger and brighter to attract lots of fireflies."

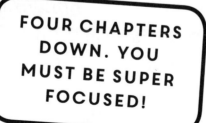

FOUR CHAPTERS DOWN. YOU MUST BE SUPER FOCUSED!

CHAPTER FIVE

DODGEBALL AND ELECTRIC EELS

GYM CAME RIGHT after lunch. It was a dodgeball day.

You know what dodgeball is, right? It's when two classes run around and throw balls at each other. Mr. Gumposer (we call him Mr. Bulldozer) picked Katie Cunningham and Burt Glass to be captains. They chose the teams. Katie picked Rosie first, which was kind of weird because Rosie isn't very good.

In the first couple of minutes of the game, Rosie, Simon, and I all got hit. We were the first three out. We did it on purpose—we had things to talk about. We sat together near the stacked gym mats by the basketball hoop.

"Okay," I said, looking around at the fifty-seven remaining kids playing dodgeball. "Anybody have any ideas?"

Rosie shook her head, but Simon spoke up quickly.

29

"I came up with something," he said confidently.

"Awesome," I said. "Let's hear it."

"Okay, we need a light that's big and bright to attract lots of fireflies, right?" Simon asked quickly. He talked fast. He had that glazy look in his eyes.

Rosie and I nodded. Ten more kids had been hit in dodgeball.

"Okay, we go to the city zoo," Simon began. "When we get there, we head straight to the electric eel tank in the Sea Life exhibit. When nobody's watching, I'll climb up to the top of the tank. Will you two hold my ankles so I don't fall in?"

We said we would—although I could tell Rosie, like me, was a little worried about where Simon's idea was going.

"Great, thanks," he said and continued.

He spoke even faster. "I'll reach into the tank and grab an electric eel. We'll hurry home and put it in a bucket of water in Molly's backyard. It will light up! Electric eels are real bright, I think. Then all the fireflies in the surrounding area will be like, 'Hey, look at that crazy-big light down there in Molly's yard! Let's go check it out!' There you go. Problem solved."

I looked out at the dodgeball game. Half the kids had been eliminated. We were running out of time.

"Umm, Simon," I said. "It's a great idea and everything, but—"

I didn't say anything else.

Because Rosie interrupted me.

"You can't grab an electric eel!" she yelled. The dodgeball game was loud, so only Simon and I heard her.

"I can't?"

"No!" Rosie exclaimed. "You'll get electrocuted!"

"Oh," Simon said and paused.

Apparently, he hadn't thought of that. "Right. Umm, bad idea."

"Plus, it needs to be firefly light," I reminded him. "It's not just *any* light that fireflies are attracted to. It's *firefly* light."

"Oh, so we need to make their actual light—you know, on their butts or whatever—brighter?" asked Simon. Rosie and I both nodded. "Well, how in the world are we going to do that?"

Rosie answered, "That's what we need to figure out."

But we weren't going to figure it out right then. The first dodgeball game was over—and the second was beginning.

"Come on," Simon said. "It's time to get hit in the head with a ball."

CHAPTER SIX

ROSIE TWIRLS HER HAIR

SCIENCE IS THE last subject on Wednesdays. Simon, Rosie, and I sat at Table 5 while Mr. Willow wrote the science fair schedule on the big whiteboard.

Simon poked me with his elbow and nodded his head toward Rosie. She was twirling her hair. That meant she was trying to figure something out.

"Mr. Willow?" Rosie called from Table 5.

SCIENCE FAIR SCHEDULE

TODAY–CHOOSE A SCIENCE FAIR PROJECT.

THURSDAY–GATHER SUPPLIES AND GET TO WORK.

FRIDAY–FINISH PROJECT.

FRIDAY NIGHT–SCIENCE FAIR!

Before even turning around, he said, "Yes, Rosie?" He knew it was Rosie. Rosie asks lots of questions during science.

Here are some examples of what Rosie has asked Mr. Willow:

"Why is the sky blue?"

"Will time travel ever be possible?"

"Why do we throw salt on sidewalks when it snows?"

This time, Rosie asked, "How does a magnifying glass work?"

37

Mr. Willow explained that a convex lens bends outward. And two convex lenses put together with both sides bent outward creates magnification. He drew the shape of it on the whiteboard. It sort of looked like a flying saucer.

Mr. Willow asked, "Why do you want to know how a magnifying glass works?"

"Just curious," Rosie answered and glanced at Katie Cunningham at Table 3 real fast. "Can you magnify light? If I shine a flashlight through a magnifying glass, will the light get bigger?"

"Hmm," Mr. Willow said and paused. This was apparently a tough question. "It wouldn't get bigger. The light would actually be more concentrated. Narrower and brighter, like a laser beam."

"Brighter?" Rosie asked. It sounded like she liked that answer.

"Brighter."

"Thank you," Rosie said.

Mr. Willow nodded and began to talk about the science fair some more.

And Rosie started to twirl her hair again. When Mr. Willow finally finished, we were able to talk to Rosie.

"Did you figure out my firefly problem?" I asked, leaning in closer.

"Did you come up with an idea for our science project?" Simon asked.

"Both," Rosie said. "We're going to build something to attract fireflies. It will be our science fair project—*and* it will get the fireflies out of Molly's head."

"That's awesome!" I exclaimed.

Simon gave Rosie a fist bump.

"But there are three problems," Rosie said. You could tell she was excited and nervous at the same time. "Three *huge* problems."

"What are they?" I asked.

"The first problem is Copycat Katie," Rosie whispered and nodded her head at Katie Cunningham. Simon and I knew exactly what Rosie was talking about. Katie had copied Rosie's science fair ideas two years in a row. "We have to keep this idea a secret."

"What's the second problem?" Simon asked.

"I don't know if we can get it done in time," Rosie answered. "We only have two days."

I asked, "And the third problem?"

"I have no idea if it will work."

Then the bell rang.

"Let's go," Simon said, reaching for his backpack on the floor. "We can talk about it on the walk home."

"I can't leave yet," Rosie whispered. She eyeballed Katie again. "I have to ask Mr. Willow one more question—but not until Katie is gone."

YOU'VE ALREADY READ SIX CHAPTERS AND 2,933 WORDS! HOW ARE YOU FEELING?

CHAPTER SEVEN

SIMON PICKS A NAME

WE WALKED TO my house from school and Rosie explained her plan to us. Simon and I thought it might actually work.

"How do we start?" I asked as we got to the back patio.

"We need to get our supplies," Rosie said as she unzipped her backpack and pulled out ten magnifying glasses. "Mr. Willow let me borrow these from the science closet. I told him they were for the science fair."

"Did he ask you what our project is?"

"Yes," Rosie answered and nodded. "But guess who came back into the room to get something from her desk right then?"

"Copycat Katie?" I asked.

Rosie squeezed her lips together, squinted her eyes, and nodded again. Rosie almost never looked mad—but she looked kind of mad right then.

"No way!" Simon exclaimed. "She wants to take your idea? Again?!"

"I didn't want to take the chance, so I told Mr. Willow I wanted it to be a surprise," Rosie said and shook the mad look off her face. She knew we had to get moving. "Let's get what we need."

"We need some big plastic bottles," Rosie said after we'd collected everything else. "Regular water bottles won't work. We need big two-liter soda bottles."

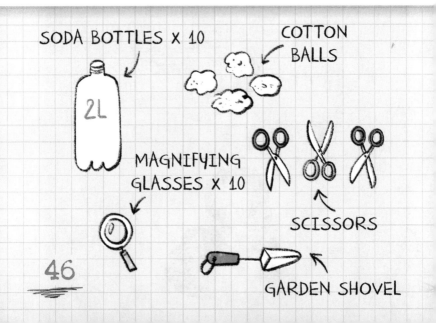

We didn't have any at my house.

But some of my neighbors did.

Simon, Rosie, and I found ten of them in the big blue recycling bins at the end of their driveways. It was kind of weird looking through my neighbors' garbage. But it wasn't gross things—like old food and wet stuff. It was just recycling things—newspapers, plastic bottles, aluminum cans, and cardboard.

We took those ten bottles back to my patio and put them with the other supplies.

"We need an awesome name for our project," Simon said.

Rosie and I thought that was a good idea.

"We're inventing something to attract fireflies," Rosie said. "What's a good name for that?"

"The Great Firefly Catcher?" I suggested.

"It's good, but we're not really catching them," Rosie said. "It's more like we're getting them to meet up in one place."

48

"I've got it!" Simon exclaimed. "The Fantastic Firefly Fetcher!"

It was perfect. Rosie and I both loved it.

"Okay, we have a name," Rosie said. "Now we have to turn these soda bottles into clear plastic tubes. Oh, and there's something else."

Simon asked, "What's that?"

"We have to figure out one more thing," Rosie said. "And it's going to be tricky."

CHAPTER EIGHT

THE TRICKY THING

WE SAT DOWN criss-cross apple-sauce on the patio to tear the bottle labels off. While we did that, Rosie told us the trickiest part of our project.

"We have to sneak into the greenhouse during school and dig ten small holes with the little shovel," Rosie said.

"We can't go outside during school," I said and bit my lip a little. "It's against the rules. We'll get in big trouble."

"That's why it's the trickiest part," Rosie said.

"We can only go outside at recess," Simon said. "But the greenhouse is locked anyway. Only teachers have keys."

"And the walls and door are made out of glass," I said, picturing the greenhouse. "It's got a screen roof to let rain in—and keep bugs and birds out—but there's no way to get inside."

"It's tricky," Rosie repeated. "But we *have* to find a way in."

SCREEN ROOF LETS RAIN IN, KEEPS BUGS AND BIRDS OUT

GLASS

LOCKED

"I have an idea," Simon said as he scratched his fingernail against a bit of label that was still stuck on his last bottle. "The walls are glass, so we can't get through them. But the top is just a screen. It's pretty loose and flimsy. I think I could get through it."

"How are you going to climb up there?" Rosie asked as we started to cut the tops and bottoms off the bottles to turn them into tubes.

"I'm not going to climb *up*," Simon said. "I'm going to fall *down*."

I asked, "How?"

"I'll jump off the roof of the school, that's how."

"You can't jump off the school roof!" Rosie screamed and laughed.

"Why not?"

53

"You'll break your legs! Or worse!" Rosie said. Now she was really laughing—like, hard. She was holding her belly.

Simon turned my way for support. He looked at me and said, "I figure the screen roof will slow me down before I smash into the ground."

I shook my head. "It won't slow you down enough. You cannot jump off the school and through the greenhouse roof."

"All right, all right," Simon said, giving up.

It was quiet then. We were each down to our last bottle to cut.

54

"We can't use the roof by falling through it," Rosie said slowly and twirled her hair, suddenly serious. "But we can use the roof."

"How?" Simon and I asked in unison.

"Tomorrow at recess," Rosie answered. She paused and looked at Simon, then at me. "We're going to play Frisbee."

MORE THAN HALFWAY THROUGH! WHAT DO YOU THINK ROSIE IS GOING TO DO WITH THE FRISBEE?

CHAPTER NINE

FRISBEE TIME

AT RECESS THE next day, Thursday, we launched our plan to get the greenhouse keys.

We hurried toward the back of the playground near the woods. That's where the school garden was. We had figured out our roles at lunch.

I would throw the Frisbee.

Rosie would negotiate with Mr. Willow. Simon would dig the holes.

Rosie and Simon watched Mr. Willow. He was the teacher on the playground with us that day. He was shooting baskets with some of the girls in my class—including Katie.

"He's not looking, Molly," Rosie said. "Go ahead and throw it. Try to get it in the middle of the roof."

I was pretty nervous. I'm not, like, totally athletic or anything. I took a deep breath—and threw the Frisbee.

57

It was a perfect shot.

Whew.

It landed near the center of the greenhouse's screen roof. We could all see it sag a little in the middle.

"Perfect throw!" Simon exclaimed.

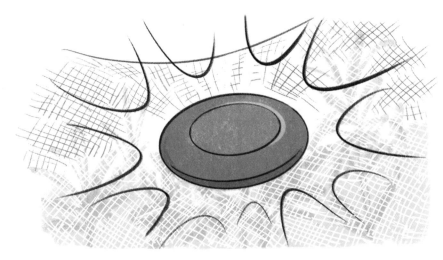

"Okay," Rosie said. "My turn. Let's hope this works."

Simon and I watched as Rosie ran over to Mr. Willow. We couldn't hear her, but we watched as she talked and motioned with her hands. She pretended to throw a Frisbee. She pointed up in the air—and at the greenhouse. She made a poking motion up toward the sky.

And then Mr. Willow did exactly what we wanted him to do. He reached into his pocket, retrieved his keys, and pointed to the one that opened the greenhouse door.

Rosie ran back.

"How fast can you dig ten holes?" Rosie asked Simon as she unlocked the glass door to the greenhouse.

"Super fast," he answered and pulled the little shovel from his back pocket.

"Great," Rosie said. She opened the door. "I told Mr. Willow that I was going to poke and nudge the Frisbee with a tomato stake to get it off the roof. I'm going to look busy,

but I'm not actually going to knock it off until you're done."

Simon nodded.

"And Molly," Rosie explained further. "You stand outside and do a lot of pointing and gesturing. Act like you're going to catch it. And spy on Mr. Willow. But don't *look* like you're spying."

"How do I do that?"

Simon said, "Just spy *casually*."

He didn't see the puzzled look on my face. He was already gone.

Rosie went into the greenhouse right after him.

Simon started to dig frantically. And Rosie started poking the Frisbee closer to the edge of the roof so it would

eventually topple over toward me. I could tell she was missing on purpose a lot.

After a few minutes, Simon called, "Five done! Five to go!"

The Frisbee was about three feet from the edge. I glanced over my shoulder as casually as I could. Mr. Willow wasn't shooting baskets anymore. His arms were crossed against his chest. He stared in our direction.

And so did Katie.

"You guys," I called and turned back around. "I think we're running out of time."

CHAPTER TEN

RUNNING OUT OF TIME

"MR. WILLOW IS staring at us!" I scream-whispered.

"Eight!" Simon yelled.

"I can see him!" Rosie scream-whispered back. "He's walking this way. And Katie's with him! She can't find out what we're doing! Hurry, Simon!"

"Nine!"

"He's halfway to us now," Rosie said

urgently—but quietly. She gave the Frisbee a good, accurate nudge and it jumped to the edge of the screen roof. About half of it hung over. "Simon, we have to go! Now!"

"Ten!" he yelled.

I felt Mr. Willow's hand on my shoulder as I stared up at the Frisbee teetering on the edge. Rosie and Simon hustled out of the greenhouse door.

Katie stood next to Mr. Willow. She totally wanted to know what we were doing, I could tell.

"Why did you just yell 'ten!' like that, Simon?" Mr. Willow asked. He didn't sound curious. He sounded like he was accusing Simon of something. It felt like we were in trouble.

I froze. I couldn't move a muscle.

"Uhh," Simon said. He didn't have an answer. I noticed that his hands were in his pockets. He was trying to hide them because they were dirty.

Rosie had an answer though. I knew she didn't like fibbing, but she couldn't give away our science fair project—especially with Katie standing right there.

"He said it would take me at least twelve pokes with the tomato stake to get the Frisbee down," she answered and turned her back toward Mr. Willow to lock the door. I saw her wrist twist as she wiggled the key. She turned back around and continued. "But I won. I got it here in ten."

She handed the keys back to Mr. Willow.

67

Mr. Willow reached up and grabbed the Frisbee for us.

"Okay, you three," Mr. Willow said as he and Katie headed back toward the basketball hoop. "Move away from the greenhouse if you're going to throw it some more."

We said we would.

When Mr. Willow and Katie and the other girls were shooting baskets again, Simon asked the question that was on my mind too.

"Rosie," he said. "How are we going to

get back in here tomorrow night before the science fair? We'll need the key again."

"No, we won't."

I asked, "Why not?"

Rosie said, "It's not locked."

"But we saw you lock it," Simon said.

"No," Rosie said and smiled. "You— and Mr. Willow—saw me turn my wrist. I never actually put the key in the handle."

Rosie is the best. The absolute best.

CHAPTER ELEVEN

CATCHING TIME

FRIDAY AT SCHOOL, we painted nine Styrofoam balls to look like the planets of our solar system. But that was just our pretend project. Obviously, our real project was about fireflies. We just didn't know if it would work.

So we did a *fake* project at school. We worked on the *actual* project at home.

After dinner, just when it started to get

dark, Simon and Rosie came to my house. We went out to my backyard. We caught as many fireflies as we could.

You can collect a LOT of fireflies in a whole hour.

And we got a ton.

We each had a mason jar with a wet cotton ball inside. That's where we put the fireflies when we caught them. Simon collected the most.

At 7:30, my mom called to us from the back door. It was time to go to the science fair.

Simon, Rosie, and I climbed into the back seat of our car. Their parents were going to meet us at the school.

"What do you have in your backpacks?" my dad asked us from the front seat.

"Just some final supplies for our project," I answered quickly. Simon's backpack was stuffed with most of the clear soda bottle tubes. Mine was jammed with a couple of the tubes and three jars full of fireflies. And Rosie's backpack held the rest of the tubes and all the magnifying glasses.

"You still don't want to tell us what it is?" Mom asked.

"Not really," I said. "It's a surprise."

"Okay," Dad said and smiled at me in the rearview mirror. "No problem."

FIREFLY
JARS ↘

SODA
↙ BOTTLE
TUBES

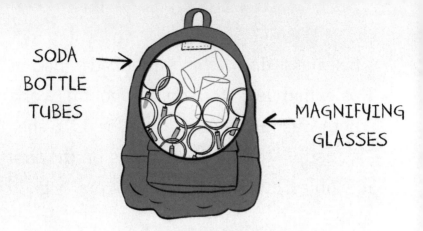

SODA BOTTLE TUBES →

← MAGNIFYING GLASSES

After we parked, Mom and Dad headed toward the school right away.

But we didn't.

"Aren't you guys coming?" Mom asked.

"We have to, umm, go over our presentation one last time," I said.

"Makes sense," responded Dad. "We'll meet you in your classroom."

I nodded. And we waited for them to go inside. We got really lucky then because no other cars pulled into the parking lot.

We sprinted across the playground, heading straight to the greenhouse.

The glass door was unlocked—just as Rosie had left it. And we got to work. There was just enough light for us to see.

A couple of fireflies escaped on the first few holes, but after that we got pretty good at it.

"I don't know, you guys," Rosie said doubtfully when we were done. "I think this might have been a bad idea.

1. I PUT ABOUT TEN FIREFLIES IN EACH HOLE.

2. ROSIE COVERED THE HOLES—AND THE FIREFLIES IN THE HOLES—REAL FAST WITH THE MAGNIFYING GLASSES.

3. SIMON STOOD A CLEAR TUBE ABOVE EACH HOLE.

75

I don't think it's going to work."

"Maybe we should wait here a few minutes," I suggested. "To see if any fireflies come."

"There's no time!" Simon yelled. "We have to go!"

We raced back to school—and hurried into the classroom.

The science fair was about to start.

ONLY TWO MORE CHAPTERS TO GO! HOW DO YOU THINK THE STORY WILL END?

CHAPTER TWELVE

TABLE 5'S TURN

OUR PLAN WAS pretty simple.

We had already asked Mr. Willow if we could be last—and he said yes. It was Simon's job to stand near the window and look out at the greenhouse every now and then. If it seemed to be getting brighter or glowing, then we'd know our firefly project had worked. And we could go outside and show it to Mr. Willow.

If it didn't, then we would show our bogus backup solar system project.

Rosie and I were super nervous. We wanted Mr. Willow to go slow to give more fireflies a chance to find the magnified light and be attracted to it.

It took about thirty minutes for Mr. Willow to look at all the other tables. There was a model of a volcano, a Mentos and Diet Coke geyser, a daffodil that had turned blue, and some other cool projects.

Mr. Willow said Katie's solar

TABLE 5

78

system model was pretty good.

"I knew she'd copy us," Rosie whispered.

I smiled and said, "But she didn't copy the right thing."

We kept looking over at Simon as Mr. Willow got closer and closer to our table.

Simon kept shrugging his shoulders. He came over once to say it was too far away to tell. He thought maybe the greenhouse was glowing a bit—but maybe not. It was so bright in the classroom, it was hard for Simon to see outside.

Mr. Willow was about thirty seconds away from our table. We looked over at Simon one last time.

He shrugged again.

"What should we do?" I whispered to Rosie.

"I don't think we should risk it," Rosie said. I could tell she was disappointed. "If we don't *know* it worked, we better just show our dumb solar system balls."

"It *might* have worked," I whispered.

"We can't risk it," Rosie whispered back. "It *could* have worked."

"We can't."

"*Maybe* it worked."

"We don't *know*," Rosie whispered and grasped the poster board that covered our Styrofoam planets.

Mr. Willow, our classmates, and all the parents gathered around Table 5.

"Okay, Table 5," Mr. Willow announced. "I'm expecting big things here."

Rosie looked down at the poster board. She knew what was behind it.

I could see the frown on her face. She was embarrassed. She didn't want to lift it up—but Rosie knew she had to.

And then Simon yelled, "Wait!"

CHAPTER THIRTEEN

MR. WILLOW'S DECISION

"WHAT IS IT, Simon?" Mr. Willow asked.

"Can we turn the lights off for a few seconds?" Simon asked loudly.

Mr. Willow tilted his head. He was curious. "Sure," he said.

One of the parents flipped the light switch.

Rosie and I snapped our heads to the left and looked outside.

It took a couple of seconds for our eyes to adjust. When they did, we could see the greenhouse.

It was glowing—and blinking.

It wasn't, like, as bright as the sun or anything, but it was definitely glowing.

"It worked!" Rosie whispered to me and squeezed my left hand. I squeezed hers back. And then Rosie pointed toward the window and in a louder voice said, "That's our science fair project!"

Everybody hurried to the classroom windows. It was easy to spot the green-yellow glow in the dark night.

"What is that?" Mr. Willow asked.

"It's our Fantastic Firefly Fetcher!" Simon yelled.

Simon, Rosie, and I led everybody outside to see it. We tried not to run, but we walked super fast across the playground to the greenhouse.

It was covered in fireflies.

Totally.

There were fireflies on all the glass walls, the door, and on the screen roof.

They were everywhere. And there were dozens—maybe hundreds—flying and blinking in the air around the greenhouse too.

Rosie explained how we made the Fantastic Firefly Fetcher to everyone. Simon and I added some details. Simon

was sure to tell everyone that he caught the most fireflies. He was proud of that.

"Is that why you got yourselves into the greenhouse yesterday?" Mr. Willow asked. "Did you throw the Frisbee up onto the roof on purpose?"

Rosie nodded. "We had to dig the holes."

"You know, you didn't have to trick me," Mr. Willow said. "I would have just let you in if you'd told me what you were doing."

"Where's the fun in that?" Simon asked. "Where's the adventure? Where's the pizzazz? Where's the chutzpah?!"

"I don't know what I'm going to do with you three," Mr. Willow said and shook his head. "You're either going to have to stay after school next week for bending the rules . . . or you're going to get first place in the science fair."

He held his hand up under his chin and looked down at the three of us.

We looked up at him. Right then a firefly fluttered down and landed on his index finger. He held it up slowly in front of his eyes. It glowed bright yellow for a couple of seconds.

And then Mr. Willow smiled.

Fun and Games!

THINK

This whole story is about attracting a ton of fireflies. What animal or insect would you want to attract? How could you do it? What would you use? Draw a picture of your plan!

FEEL

Think about how fireflies fly around. They hover sometimes, but they also dip and dart in every direction. Can you move like a firefly? Do it by yourself—how do you feel? Now do it in front of someone else—how do you feel?

ACT

Molly, Rosie, and Simon get most of the supplies for their science project from the recycling bin. What can you make using the stuff that's inside your recycling bin?

Tom Watson is the author of the popular STICK DOG and STICK CAT series. And now he's the author of this new series, TROUBLE AT TABLE 5. Tom lives in Chicago with his wife and kids and their big dog, Shadow. When he's not at home, Tom's usually out visiting classrooms all over the country. He's met a lot of students who remind him of Molly, Simon, and Rosie. He's learned that kids are smarter than adults. Like, way smarter.

Marta Kissi is originally from Warsaw but now lives in London where she loves bringing stories to life. She shares her art studio with her husband, James, and their pet plant, Trevor.